# DEVELOPING EMOTIONAL INTELLIGENCE

## 30 Ways for Teens and Young Adults to Develop Their Caring Capabilities

ISRAELIN SHOCKNESS

**Successful Youth Living - Vol. 3**

VAN QUEST PUBLISHING
motivating | inspiring | educating

**Cataloguing-in-Publication Data**

Israelin Shockness

Includes bibliographical references

**DEVELOPING EMOTIONAL INTELLIGENCE**

**30 Ways for Older Teens and Young Adults to Develop Their Caring Capabilities – Vol. 3**

ISBN: 978-1-7750094-5-0 (paperback)

ISBN: 978-1-7750094-0-5 (Ebook)

SERIES- Successful Youth Living - Vol. 3

# DISCLAIMER

All material provided in this book is for information purposes only and should not be taken as a substitute for professional, psychological, or mental health advice. It is intended to encourage and motivate you to think and to have meaningful conversations around these issues, the objective being to promote more responsible behavior at all times. If, for any reason, you feel you are experiencing any emotional or other crisis, you are encouraged to seek out professional care. References have been made to peer-reviewed and other research studies and works, but this is not intended to imply specific endorsement of this author's work by any of these authors and professionals mentioned. The opinions expressed in this book are solely those of this author.

# PURPOSE OF THIS SERIES

*Successful Youth Living* is a series of books, dealing with issues, which older teens and young adults face as they go through the uncertainty of adolescence. A few of the topics dealt with are: becoming a leader in your own right without being a bully; learning how to assume responsibility; fostering positive attitudes and habits for self-growth; learning how to continue your education regardless of where you stopped or whether you dropped out; developing emotional intelligence and caring for self and others; learning how to deal with stress; recognizing the importance of personal reflection; and being a person that others admire for the right reasons.

The 'seed' for these volumes was actually planted when the author, then a teenager on a scholarship, almost dropped out of university because of her inability to deal with many issues that had nothing to do with school. Thanks to the insightfulness and mentorship of a professor, the author became a teen mentor and since then have committed herself to paying it forward by looking out for vulnerable teens and young adults that have lost their way, the way she had almost lost hers. After years of further study, a career as an educator working with children, teens and young adults, years as a volunteer in marginalized communities and as a columnist in a weekly community newspaper, Israelin has recognized that many of the issues plaguing adolescents have not changed. She has therefore decided to share ideas she has gleaned from personal experience, as well as from her students, readers, studies, and from peer-reviewed articles.

The hope is that these ideas would be a catalyst for thinking and discussion among teens and young adults, preparing them for making split-minute decisions that they may face in the future.

# DEDICATION

This book is dedicated to all young people, both those who are transitioning from adolescence to adulthood and those who are still finding their way in their adult role. For the younger ones, this can be a confusing period because of the physical, emotional, intellectual, cognitive, and social changes that are taking place in their lives. For older ones, adolescence is a time of trying on new roles. This 'trying on' of roles is individual and unique. Whether younger or older, adolescents are continually engaging in a balancing act, between being a child that is dependent and being an adult that is independent, and at times, not knowing which role they should assume.

One thing is clear. Young people strive to learn what is socially acceptable, while at the same time wanting to be authentic in their own right. One of the challenges some young people have is that of showing emotions, because for many this is something that children do, and as adolescents and young adults, this is something that they have to control.

Yet, a better understanding of emotional intelligence reveals that it is something that all individuals need. It does not matter whether you are male or female, teenager, young adult, or even older adult, emotional intelligence is important for future everyday success, even as important as cognitive development. Emotional intelligence is critical, for it is the ability to understand and manage your emotions so that you can effectively communicate and empathize with others. It is through this ability that you will be better able to interact with others in your family, in your work setting, in your school, and in your dealings with others in society. It is an ability that is fundamental to everything else you will do in the future.

Therefore, the chapters in this volume address many of the ways in which emotional intelligence feature in the lives of young people, and in the things they find challenging. These chapters give readers the opportunity to ponder these challenges before they have to deal with them. While much of the information and discussion in this book has been drawn from real life experiences and conversations with adolescents, many of them students, some information has been gleaned from peer-reviewed articles as well as from personal experience. Some articles have been provided as further reading.

My hope is that these different chapters will serve as a catalyst for greater consideration and discussion of the many issues raised. It is also my hope that these chapters may serve as a source of knowledge, with young people recognizing that knowledge is power.

Carry this knowledge and power forward by not only reading these chapters, thinking for yourselves, seeing how the issues and scenarios apply or relate to you, but also by discussing these issues with your family members and friends.

There is nothing more empowering than communicating and sharing your ideas with others, and expanding your own horizons on a variety of topics. The result will be empowerment to take and maintain control of your life and the ability to help others to do the same.

**SUCCESSFUL YOUTH LIVING – VOL. 3**

**DEVELOPING EMOTIONAL INTELLIGENCE -**
*30 Ways for Older Teens and Young Adults to Develop Their Caring Capabilities*

# TABLE OF CONTENTS

# TAKING RESPONSIBILITY FOR WHAT IS EMOTIONAL INTELLIGENCE?

Think about it. You are standing in a room with many friends that you know, and another friend comes in, speaks to most of you, makes fun about the things that you did with her a few days ago, and she completely ignores that one friend who is standing with you. You know that friend standing with you is often ostracized because she is from a different country and many of the people from your school leave her out of activities. You notice that this friend from a different country is feeling completely embarrassed, because of the slight and the fact that she is left out of the conversation. You notice it and it bothers you, so you look for an opportunity to bring this friend into the conversation. You are able to make her feel that she is part of the group. You are quite likely a person with emotional intelligence.

Emotional intelligence is often defined as an ability and/or as a trait that allows an individual to perceive, understand, use, and manage emotions, both in himself/herself and in others. This means that an emotionally intelligent person would be able to pick up on the facial cues of others, which reveal their emotions. Also, an emotionally intelligent person would be aware of how his or her own body reveals emotions, would understand his or her own emotions and the emotions of others, and would be able to identify the factors that contribute to these emotions. Being aware of these emotions would help to enhance critical thought in this individual.

Perceiving, understanding, and using these emotions to promote critical thought, the emotionally intelligent individual would then be able to regulate his or her own emotions in order to suit the circumstances.

## EXAMPLE

An emotionally intelligent person who may have recognized circumstances that are unpleasant to another by reading the facial cues and subtle behaviors of that other person would very likely become aware of and understand how that other person is feeling. Recognizing this, the emotionally intelligent individual may then take action that would change the circumstances and the emotions of the other person. By being able to put himself or herself in the other person's position, the emotionally intelligent person can change the emotions of the other person. This is what you did when you found a way to bring your friend into the conversation and help her to be part of the group.

## BEING ABLE TO LISTEN TO OTHERS AND FEEL WITH THEM

Someone who is emotionally intelligent would therefore be able to understand other people's emotions, and be able to express his or her own feelings in empathizing with others. This may sometimes involve being able to listen to other people and being able to feel with them. It means not being selfish and not just focusing on one's emotions.

## DIMENSIONS OF EMOTIONAL INTELLIGENCE

Emotional intelligence is therefore said to be made up of self-awareness, empathy, handling emotions, managing feelings, and having the motivation to consider one's emotions and the emotions of others. A person who is emotionally intelligent would be able to get along with others well, because he or she would be able to take other people's feelings into consideration. Through empathizing with others, the emotionally intelligent person would be able to understand what the other person is going through and what that person needs at that time to feel better. It would also mean that the emotionally intelligent person would understand how other people's emotions are affecting him or her and how to change the circumstances.

## CAPABILITIES OF EMOTIONAL INTELLIGENCE

Emotional intelligence has also been said to be made up of seven capabilities, namely, knowing our feelings, controlling our emotions, exploring our incentives, recognizing other peoples' emotions, and handling relationships to make sure that all is well.

## THE VALUE OF EMOTIONAL INTELLIGENCE

Emotional intelligence therefore allows the individual who possesses this capacity to be able to empathize with others and to understand what is taking place in his or her environment, and where possible take action to improve relations.

## CAN EMOTIONAL INTELLIGENCE BE LEARNED?

While there are those who hold that emotional intelligence is a trait that an individual has as an integral part of his or her personality, there are others who see emotional intelligence as an ability that can be learned. As Joshith (2012) points out: "The fact is that emotional intelligence can be nurtured, developed, and augmented. It is not a trait that we either have or don't have. We can increase our emotional intelligence at any time in our lives as well as learn and practice the skills that make up the concept of emotional intelligence" (p. 56).

## TRAIT AND ABILITY?

Some would point out that emotional intelligence is both a trait and an ability, and that there are some people who are naturally emotionally intelligent, while others may be mildly so, and others who could develop this capacity as a result of being nurtured and taught. In this case, some would conclude that emotional intelligence is both a trait and an ability.

## MUCH BROADER LIGHT

However, some see emotional intelligence in a much broader light, and define it as "the mental usage of emotions, and it includes individual awareness, the ability to manage emotions, self-motivation, and developing effective communication skills" (Ortug, 2013, p. 81). Some see emotional intelligence as self-awareness, as the ability to control our emotions (self-management), and to control emotions to achieve a certain objective or a goal. Emotional intelligence is also seen as the ability to recognize other people's emotions, or to have empathy. It also involves handling interpersonal relations and demonstrating skill in handling other people's feelings. These are skills that lead to popularity, leadership ability, and interpersonal success. (Goleman, Ioannidou & Konstantikaki, 2008).

## CHAPTER 1 - REFERENCES AND FURTHER READING

What is Emotional Intelligence? Ioannidou, F. & Konstantikaki, V. (2008). Empathy as emotional intelligence: What is it really about? *International Journey of Caring Services, 1*(3), 118-123.

Joshith, V. P. (2012). Emotional intelligence as a tool for innovative learning. *I-Manager's Journal on Educational Psychology, 5*(4), 54-60.

Schutte, N. S., Malouff, J. M. & Thorsteinsson, E. B. (2013). Increasing emotional intelligence through training: Current status and future directions. *The International Journal of Emotional Education, 5*(1), 56-72

Thompson, R. A. (2003). Counseling techniques: Improving relationships with others, ourselves, our families, and our environment. Brunner Routledge.

Yale Center for Emotional Intelligence (2013). Emotions matter. Yale University. Retrieved from *http://eiyale.wpengine.com/wp-content/uploads/2013/07/YaleCenter_EmotionsMatter.pdf*

Zeidner, M., Matthews, G. & Roberts, R.D. (2009). What we know about emotional intelligence: how it affects learning, work, relationships, and our mental health. Boston: MIT Press.

# CHAPTER 2

# THE IMPORTANCE OF EMPATHY

Imagine this! You have a job at a big-box store, and you are also a student. Employees are not allowed to miss their shifts or to refuse to work when they are asked to do so. The punishment is usually that these employees would not be scheduled to fill regular shifts, which means that they can be denied adequate work for the month and so are unable to meet your basic living expenses. One of the employees in my section has a sick mother and so has missed some shifts because of having to rush her mother to the emergency. While she was excused once before, the second time it happened, she was threatened with dismissal. Since this location is not unionized, there is nothing that this employee can do. Loss of her job would be catastrophic, since she is dependent on it for taking care of her family.

You have heard of her plight and understand the difficulty that she must be facing. Therefore, you met with her one day and told her that if she is ever faced with the predicament that she has to take her mother to the emergency and cannot come in to work, that you would fill in for her. She is very thankful for this offer.

You have demonstrated that you have emotional intelligence and that you are able to empathize with this woman. You have demonstrated that you understand what this young woman must be going through.

Empathy is a quality that is often associated with true caring. It has been described as the capacity to understand another's "state of mind" or emotion. It is described as the ability to "put oneself into another's shoes," or in some way "experience the outlook or emotions of another being within oneself" (Ioannidou & Konstantikaki, 2008, p. 118).

## WHEN YOU EMPATHIZE

Many young people find themselves in the situation where they may feel despondent and discouraged. Knowing that there is someone else who understands what they are going through is very important. When someone empathizes with another person, the situation does not always have to be one of sorrow or misery; it could be one of joy, excitement or other emotions. Being able to empathize is being able to feel with the other person, which has been pointed out earlier as having emotional intelligence. While some see empathy as a skill, some see it as a trait that someone possesses.

## EMPATHY AND COMMUNICATION

If we are to communicate effectively, we must have a measure of empathy. In fact, it has been pointed out that empathy and confidence form the basis "on which any effective relationship, understanding and communication can be built" (Ioannidou & Konstantikaki, 2008, p. 119). This is evident for empathy is necessary to understand other people's feelings and ideas. If we are unable to understand how others feel and what their ideas are, we lack the common basis on which to communicate. We would be having a different understanding of what is being discussed, thereby making it difficult for communication to take place.

## EMPATHY AND PROBLEM-SOLVING

When people face common problems, they have to have a common understanding as to what those problem are. This comes about when they are able to listen to each other and understand what each other stands for, even though they may differ on certain issues. In trying to arrive at a solution, people have to be able to listen to each other, to understand how each other feels, and empathize with each other. It is by a common understanding of what each person wants that in most cases a compromise could be achieved and a solution reached. Empathy is therefore critical in engaging in problem-solving, and helps to prevent conflicts or to reduce these. If individuals lack the ability to empathize, this could be a major stumbling block to finding solutions.

## EMPATHY AND TEAMWORK

Teamwork involves different individuals trying to achieve certain objectives by cooperating to achieve these objectives. This means that individuals have to learn to listen to each other, and on the basis of this listening, understand what each other's requirements are. It also means understanding the emotions that each team member has. It is with this in mind that members of a team come to appreciate each other's feelings and can cooperate to solve problems, bearing in mind the emotional needs of each member.

## RELATIONSHIP BETWEEN EMPATHY AND VIOLENCE

Several studies have shown that young people who engage in violent behavior demonstrate very little empathy. Young people who reported having high levels of exposure to violence also reported having low levels of empathy. It was also noted that young people who were exposed to high levels of violence in their communities and who also had low level of empathy were also found to use violence frequently. Studies revealed that having low empathy alone was not seen as a factor predicting violence, but when low empathy was associated with high levels of community violence, this was seen as highly predictive that the young people who were exposed to this violence were likely to be involved in violence themselves.

## EMPATHY AS AN ANTIDOTE TO VIOLENCE

Some suggestion was made that families can help to inoculate their children against violent behaviour by promoting the development of empathy among family members. While this was something that could be encouraged among young children, it was shown that it was also possible to develop empathy among adolescents, through training that brought about attitude change.

## DEVELOPING EMPATHY IN THE YOUNG

One strategy that some people use to promote empathy is having a pet within the family, and thereby teaching children and young people how to care for their pets, and by extension how to show caring towards others. At the same time, some parents have recognized the low level of empathy their children have by the way they treat their pets.

# CHAPTER 2: REFERENCES AND FURTHER READING

Holt, S. & Marques, J. (2012). Empathy in leadership: Appropriate or misplaced? An empirical study on a topic that is asking for attention. *Journal of Business Ethics, 105*(1), 95-105.

Ingram, J. & Cengemi, J. (2012). Emotions, emotional intelligence and leadership: A brief, pragmatic perspective. *Education*, Summer.

Ioannidou, F. & Konstantikaki, V. (2008). Empathy as emotional intelligence: What is it really about? *International Journey of Caring Services, 1*(3), 118-123.

Irimia, C. (2010). Empathy as a source of attitude change. Contemporary *Readings in Law and Social Justice, 2*(2), 319-324.

Moble, T., Kloem, S. & Rehbein, F. (2014). Longitudinal effects of violent media usage on aggressive behavior: The significance of empathy. *Societies, 4*(1), 105-124.

Palmeri, S., D. & Truscott, S. D. (2004). Empathy, exposure to community violence, and use of violence among urban, at-risk adolescents. *Child & Youth Care Forum, 33*(1), 33-50.

Pavlovich, K. & Krahnke, K. (2012). Empathy, connectedness, and organisation. *Journal of Business Ethics, 105*(1), 131-137.

Rogers, K. (2004). Building activities for Young Students. *Strategies, 17*(4), 17-19.

Swick, K. (2005). Preventing violence through empathy development in families. *Early Childhood Education Journal, 33*(1), 53-59.

# CHAPTER 3

# CONFLICT RESOLUTION AND EMOTIONAL INTELLIGENCE

How do you deal with your emotions? Are you moody? Do things bother you easily? Do you find it easy controlling your emotions? At times, do you feel out of control? How do you deal with conflict? Do you find it easy resolving conflicts? These are some of the questions that may come to mind as you think about emotional intelligence and how it affects you. Learning about the relationship between conflict resolution and emotional intelligence will help you answer some of these questions.

One of the dimensions of emotional intelligence is being able to manage one's feelings. Many of the feelings that young people reportedly experience on a regular basis include anger, anxiety, mood disorders, impulse-control disorders, and more. When some of these feelings become strong enough, the result is often violence as the young persons involved may move to hurt those that cause them these negative feelings.

Several methods are used for dealing with these feelings, and in many instances, expert attention is needed to help children and young people deal with these. In instances like these, it is highly recommended that young people with these difficult situations speak to an adult that can lead them to the appropriate professional, if such is required to help them sort out their feelings and emotions.

## DEALING WITH CONFLICTS

One of the problems we face in the 21st century, and which society has always faced, is how to deal with conflicts. Several theories have been put forward for defusing conflicts and for helping individuals to come to reasonable solutions, where people on different sides of an issue accept the outcome. When solutions are reached, when only one side is very pleased with the outcome, invariably the other side is very dissatisfied. This is why one of the common approaches that is promoted is that of the win-win solution.

## WIN-WIN SOLUTION

Do you seek out a win-win solution, or do you try to resolve the conflict, so that you win. While many people would want to have things their way, there are times when it is important to consider that the other person would want the same thing. But this cannot happen, so there has to be a compromise.

This is based on the idea that the parties involved have to come to a common understanding of the situation, where both parties have taken the feelings of each other into consideration. Emotional intelligence is apparent here as both parties perceive the cues given, understand what is at stake, use their understanding of each other's emotions, and manage their emotions to suit the circumstances. With emotional intelligence, the ability to pick up on cues, you will have an understanding of what the other person wants, and so be able to come to a middle ground where both of you can feel that you have gained something, although you would also have to give up something.

## DEFUSING A CONFLICT SITUATION

In many instances conflicts develop between friends and lead to negative feelings. Not being able to resolve these conflicts could be detrimental to the friendship over time. If you are to salvage your friendship, you would have to overcome the negative feelings and resolve the conflict.

## DEALING WITH NEGATIVE FEELINGS

There are some ways of dealing with negative feelings by learning how to be empathic and to build positive relationships. One of the ways is to put yourself in the place of the other person. Think of what may have been going through your mind if you were in the other person's place. Maybe that other person is feeling just that way. Ask yourself, "Is there anything I can do or say to change a negative feeling that the other person may be experiencing, especially if the negative feelings came about because of something I did or said?"

## WHEN YOU ARE THE CAUSE OF NEGATIVE FEELINGS

In some cases, by recognizing that you may have been the cause of negative feelings of another person, you can say something that could change the meaning of a previous word or action that gave the wrong meaning. Maybe, the meaning that you intended was communicated, but you regret having said it. Emotional intelligence would reveal the negative effects your words had, and would also reveal that you are in a position to try and change the effects. By addressing the situation straight on, apologizing for your insensitive comments, and explaining that what you said or done was because you were angry, then you may have the opportunity to defuse this difficult situation or conflict. At this point, your friend may realize that you were really trying to get even by making your insensitive comment and may accept your apology. However, developing your emotional intelligence would help you prevent these situations from occurring. Being sensitive to your friend's feelings in the first place would have made you aware of the comments you would have made.

## IT WORKS IN OTHER SETTINGS, TOO

Groups or individuals who differ on issues could strive for a better understanding of each other's feelings, and seek a compromise through greater emotional intelligence. In some work settings, conflicts may rise, but according to Friedman (2016), there are two channels of interaction in a work setting. Drawing on the work of Dr. Suchman, Friedman identifies these channels as the task channel and the relationship channel. The task channel refers to the work that is to be done, and sometimes, co-workers disagree on how something is to be done. On the other hand, there is the relationship channel. In some situations, these two channels could become crossed when there is disagreement in the work environment. These are generally difficult problems that seem incapable of being resolved.

## SEPARATING OUT THE CHANNELS

Not liking a co-worker, you may be inclined to disagree with a position that he supports. It is possible that you may not have considered the position that he holds, primarily because you do not like him, or because you had a conflict with him some time earlier. How would you deal with this?

This inability to resolve a problem sometimes comes about because the two people trying to come to a solution have had difficult relations or conflicts earlier on. This could be the situation with you and your co-worker. It may not be that you dislike him, but maybe you are still upset about something that he did or said. As one author points out, "It's when we get the two channels crossed that our ability to collaborate constructively suffers. One approach to reducing tension during disagreements involves deliberately attending to the relational channel and reaffirming your commitment to the relationship" (Friedman, 2016).

## EMOTIONAL INTELLIGENCE TO THE RESCUE

Having emotional intelligence would help you deal effectively with this situation. Emotional intelligence allows one individual to recognize that these two channels are becoming crossed, and to make the decision to try to defuse the conflict. Friedman (2016) recommends that the person who recognizes the crossing of the two channels take the initiative to reduce the tension. "One approach to reducing tension during disagreements involves deliberately attending to the relational channel and reaffirming your commitment to the relations. This way there's no confusion about what the argument is really about. By momentarily focusing on the relationship, you disentangle the personal from the business" (Friedman, 2016). By removing the personal tension from the situation, you are then able to deal with the problem.

## USING RELATIONSHIP-BUILDING STATEMENTS

The approach therefore calls for the one person to make "relationship-building statements" such as pointing out that he or she really wants to work with the other person with whom he or she is having the disagreement, or making statements such as "I can feel your enthusiasm as you talk", "You clearly put a lot of work into this," or "I've always appreciated your creativity" and the like (Friedman, 2016). In this way, the one person with emotional intelligence uses it to show the other that the disagreement that the two are having is not about the relationship, but about the task. At this point, the two could then move ahead to deal with the task at hand. This is a particularly good approach that you can use, particularly if you are part of a team, where the conflict developed between you and a team mate, and where you need to work on a team problem.

# CHAPTER 3: REFERENCES AND FURTHER READING

Bellafiore, D. (2016). Interpersonal conflict and effective communication. Retrieved from *http://www.drbalternatives.com/articles/cc2.html*

Fitzgibbons, R. P. (2015). Protecting the emotional health of children. Marital Healing Institute. Retrieved from *http://www.maritalhealing.com/conflicts/conflicts inchildren.php*

Friedman, R. (January 12, 2016). Defusing an emotionally charged conversation with a colleague. Harvard Business Review. Retrieved from *https://hbr.org/2016/01/defusing-an-emotionally-charged-conversation-with-a-colleague*

Joshith, V. P. (2012). Emotional intelligence as a tool for innovative learning. *I-Manager's Journal on Educational Psychology, 5*(4), 54-60.

Matthews, G., Roberts, R. D., & Zeidner, M. (2009). What we known about emotional intelligence: How it affects learning, work, relationship, and our mental health. Boston: MIT Press.

Ortug, Z. (2013). Managing emotions in the workplace: Its mediating effect on the relationship between organizational trust and occupational stress. *International Business Research, 6*(4), 81-88.

Pavlovich, K. & Krahnke, K. (2012). Empathy, connectedness, and organisation. *Journal of Business Ethics, 105*(1), 131-137.

CHAPTER 4

# EDUCATION OF THE HEART

When we speak of 'education', we refer primarily to the act of gaining more knowledge. It refers to academic improvement or improvement of the mind. I was very intrigued by a discussion I heard when the Dalai Lama met with Bishop Desmond Tutu, Professor Joanne Archibald, a First Nations' scholar, and some Nobel Prize winners at a roundtable discussion at the Pacific Coliseum in Vancouver some years ago. The Dalai Lama raised the topic of the 'education of the heart'.

According to the Buddhist leader of Tibet, what our world needs now more than anything else is "balancing the education of the mind with the education of the heart." He pointed out that we have been observing very educated world leaders with little human feeling interacting with violence on the global stage. The Dalai Lama explained that these leaders show that "human knowledge without the proper balance of a good and warm heart brings more unhappiness." But he argued that through our intelligence as well as our compassion, we could use laws and other methods to increase and sustain our values. Each of us has the potential for great compassion.

## OUR SCHOOLS DON'T DO IT

In the 21st century, this argument for the "education of the heart" is even more urgent, considering the level of violence in speech and actions on the world stage, and in many unexpected places. Yet, our modern society does not stress education of the heart as part of our educational process. We relegate this to our religious institutions, even though we do not allow some of these institutions to be effective, because we condemn them as irrational. We also keep most of these religions out of the schools. Also, by criticizing these institutions, we take the force of the message out of their teachings.

## VIOLENCE AND HATRED NOT FODDER FOR EDUCATION OF THE HEART

By the same token, many religious institutions have become so extreme that there is no place for education of the heart. Rather, some teach violence and hatred locally and on a global scale, under the guise of nationalism and racial superiority, while others teach these destructive practices under the guise of religious fundamentalism and religious fervor.

Many of our politicians provide bad examples of human caring and compassion, and actually reinforce bullying and racial hatred. Consequently, education of the heart receives very little attention, and is given very little credibility.

## WHAT IT TAKES TO BE A HUMAN BEING?

Bishop Tutu, addressing the issue of the education of the heart, pointed out that the highest praise one could lavish on a person in his country of South Africa is to say that person has "what it takes to be a human being." As the bishop elaborated, a person is only a human being because of his or her humanity in dealing with others. It is by being 'gentle,' 'compassionate,' 'hospitable,' and 'wanting to share' that we show our caring and humanity for others. Our humanity is therefore closely bound up with the humanity of others. It is the ability to connect emotionally with others, to demonstrate emotional intelligence at work. Therefore, when we dehumanize others, we dehumanize ourselves, and demonstrate a paucity of emotional intelligence.

## TRADITIONS AND VALUES OF OUR ELDERS

Professor Archibald, speaking about education of the heart in terms of First Nations' people, recognized the importance of the values of their ancestors. She explained that in her community it is important to pass on the traditions and values of the older to the younger generations. This is why the elders in indigenous cultures encourage each person to hold in their 'hearts, memories, and mind' those values that are important to their culture and to take responsibility for passing these on to the younger people.

## COMPASSION, FORGIVENESS, AND HUMANITY

What the Dalai Lama and other members of the roundtable discussion pointed out was that values and traditions were important in promoting education of the heart. Bishop Tutu was asked how is it possible in South Africa to bring together groups that see each other as enemies, without trying to force them to interact. The bishop illustrated how the education of the heart could accomplish this. He told of the case of a massacre in South Africa in which 40 Blacks were killed by some white police officers. A meeting was called and the room was filled with angry people on both sides.

Then, one white officer acknowledged: "We gave the order to shoot." According to Bishop Tutu, the tension rose so high that one could feel it. Then the officer, who had acknowledged the police giving the order, made the plea: "Please forgive us." The power of the education of the heart prevailed, as the room erupted in applause. As Bishop Tutu reiterated, "You can't force anyone to be penitent and confess." It is through compassion, forgiveness and humanity that we could turn ugliness into beauty, and transform violence into peace. It is through emotional intelligence that these two groups were able to appreciate the feelings of members of each group, and were able to bring about a reconciliation.

## RELEVANT TO OUR PRESENT SITUATION –
## POLICE SHOOTINGS

This seems to have much relevance to what is taking place in our society. With vigilantism, citizen muggings, and police shootings, people are angry, bitter, and easy to use violence. While we are stressing education of the mind, we are overlooking education of the heart, the development of compassion, forgiveness, humanity, and the use of reason and gentleness. This applies to all concerned.

## PAY ATTENTION TO THE MESSAGE

In our schools, in our community organizations, and in our homes, all of us, both old and young, need to temper our knowledge of the material world and our scientific accomplishments with compassion and humanity. We need to pay attention to the message that Bishop Tutu so poignantly put forward, that when we dehumanize others, we dehumanize ourselves. We need to follow the example of the First Nations' people as Prof. Archibald maintained, that of passing on our values from generation to generation, and we need to stress the education of the heart, as the Dalai Lama and others at the roundtable discussion encouraged. But what all of these leaders have said is not something new, but rather something that has attracted the attention of the ancient philosophers, but which has been overlooked for far too long. This is evident in a quote from Aristotle, the Greek philosopher from the 4th century B.C.: "Educating the mind without educating the heart is no education at all."

## EDUCATING OUR MINDS

Young people everywhere can think about ways to educate their hearts. Consider all the ways you can be kind and compassionate to those around you. This does not make you weak. It only makes you more humane in the way you relate to others. It shows that you are a person that is concerned about others, that you are not selfish, but that you can be generous and help others that are in need. It also shows that you are capable of caring for others without looking for something in return.

# CHAPTER 4: *REFERENCES AND FURTHER READING*:

Gardner, H. (1983). Frames of Mind: The Theory of Multiple Intelligences. New York: Basic Books.

Lipsitz, J. (1995). Prologue: why should we care about caring? *Phi Delta Kappan, 76*(9)

Stomfay-Stitz, A. & Wheeler, E. (2002). Caring is at the heart of peace education. *Childhood Education, 78*(5).

Swick, K. J. & Freeman, N. K. (2004). Nurturing peaceful children to create a caring world: The role of families and communities. *Childhood Education, 81*(1).

Wilson, S. M. & Ferch, S. T. (2005). Enhancing resilience in the workplace through the practice of caring relationships. *Organization Development Journal, 23*(4), 45-60.

Yale Center for Emotional Intelligence (2013). Emotions Matter. Yale University. Retrieved from *http://eiyale.wpengine.com/wp-content/uploads/2013/07/YaleCenter_EmotionsMatter.pdf*

CHAPTER 5

# TRYING TO UNDERSTAND AGGRESSION AND VIOLENCE

## PERSONAL EXPERIENCE

Engaging in a conversation with seven young men between the ages of 14 and 15 a few summers ago, I found that one of the main themes that came up quite frequently in our discussions was that of being a man. I also noted that in our discussion another underlying theme that came up quite frequently was that of violence. When I eventually asked what they perceived as "manhood", I got several answers, but the main idea was "getting respect," not taking any insults or 'put downs' from anyone, and at times having "to teach the other person a lesson." This often meant engaging in a fight, because, according to one of these young men, to "allow someone to insult you and not do anything about it" was "totally unacceptable" and tantamount to cowardice. The young men felt that to be disrespected and to not do anything about it would ruin their 'reputation'. What I found was that everyone wanted to be thought of as being 'tough', for that was what they saw being a man was all about.

## APOLOGY GIVEN, BUT NOT ACCEPTED

During this meeting, one young man, to taunt another, jokingly made the remark, "Your mother." Although this appears as a simple statement, in certain cultures it is a loaded one. The other young man, taking this as an insult about his mother, who happened to have been recently deceased, threatened to hurt the other. He would not accept an apology, although the offending young man, realizing his mistake, offered one. All I could have done to ease the tension was to insist on an apology anyway. The offending young man did offer an apology, but it was such a half-hearted gesture that I sensed that this was not going to be the end of this matter. To avoid a confrontation, I dismissed the young men at different times during the afternoon.

## MANHOOD AND VIOLENCE

In trying to explain the incidence of violence among young people in our society, theorists provide several explanations. Some theories explain violence in terms of societal factors, namely, poverty, discrimination, and failure of our education system. Others speak of dangerous neighborhoods (broken windows) that present the opportunity for crime. Other factors highlighted as contributing to violence among young people include high incidence of unemployment, lack of marketable skills, breakdown of the family, and the influence of the mass media through TV violence and music lyrics. Discrimination is also a factor, although not a necessary one for criminality, since there are some individuals who are not discriminated against, who are not of a specific race or ethnicity, and who display criminal behavior.

## NO ONE SINGLE FACTOR LEADS TO CRIMINALITY

Yet, none of these factors by themselves is sufficient to lead one into criminal behavior. We may also add into the equation the existence of gangs, the accessibility to guns, the easy money that may be available from involvement in the drug trade, the widespread use of drugs and alcohol, mental instability, and impulsivity. These factors provide a menu for violent crime, especially among youth.

## MORE VIOLENCE AMONG MALES THAN FEMALES

Research has shown that there is a greater incidence of aggression and violence among males than females, and although there are few studies that point to hormonal differences between the genders, there are far more studies that point to socialization or social learning. Research has shown that the socialization of males has been associated with violence. As Carlo, Raffaele, Laible and Meyer (1999) contend, "males are exposed to parenting practices that promote rough-and-tumble, physically aggressive behaviors, whereas females are exposed to parenting practices that promote caring and close interpersonal relationships."

## BIOLOGICAL FACTORS?

James Gilligan (2010) also point to biological factors that may contribute to males being more violent. He is quoted as saying: "The only two innate biological variables that do appear to be among determinants of violent behavior are youth and maleness. These patterns are universal across cultures, historical epochs, and social circumstances." The explanation seems to be that males possess the sex hormones and biological predispositions that make them aggressive and violent.

## INADEQUATE EXPLANATION?

However, appeal to biological explanations for differences in violence is often problematic, as these explanations are often used to support theories of inequality between males and females and among people of different ethnicities. It is on this basis that biological explanations of differences are often discarded.

## EMOTIONS IMPORTANT

Yet, living in the 21st century, in one of the most developed civilizations, one would expect that young people, males and females alike, are able to display greater humanity one towards the other. It is also expected that young men and young women, imbued with reason, should be able to express themselves verbally without having to resort to physical force.

## BETTER SOCIAL RELATIONS

Research has also shown that young people that have had better relations with their peers over the years tend to know how to relate to others in a variety of social situations. In fact, as Tate (2001) explains, "poor peer relationships were closely associated with social cognitive skills deficits." Failure to form relationships with their peers could lead to serious problems, while "quality friendships are indicative of children's developmental mastery and serve as a protective factor for those at risk for concurrent and future difficulties" (Ronk, Hund, & Landau, 2011).

## SOCIOLOGICAL AND PSYCHOLOGICAL FACTORS LINKED TO CRIMINAL BEHAVIOR

In short, there are many sociological and psychological factors that can be linked to criminal behavior, particularly among youth. The fact that some of these factors are present in a young person's life does not mean that this young person would automatically enter a life of violence and aggression. It is a very individual matter.

## ADDRESSING VIOLENCE AND AGGRESSION ON DIFFERENT LEVELS

I believe that mitigating aggression and violence has to take place on different levels. On a societal level, it has to involve finding ways to deal with some of these factors that lead to criminality. However, on an individual level, people have to take personal responsibility and exercise self-control. Despite the environment in which a young person lives, the emotions that the young person feels inside is going to make a major difference in how he or she responds to that environment. This is why, coming from the same environment, some people make it and others don't.

### PERSONAL RESPONSIBILITY

Although our society is expected to provide the environment in which every individual can thrive, when the society fails the individual, the individual must not fail himself or herself. Personal responsibility becomes even more important under these circumstances.

## EXERCISE SELF-CONTROL

Since youth violence has been identified as a matter that should be focused on, the message to young people is to try to exercise self-control. When things seem really dismal, nerves may become frayed, and the slightest provocation could appear as a major annoyance. Try to keep a perspective on things. Nothing is worth engaging in criminal behavior, and starting on a road of crime. It leads nowhere.

## WHAT IS CAUSING SO MUCH STRESS?

As an intelligent young person, think things out. See what is causing you so much stress. Are you stressed because you have no way of making a living? Are you involved with people that you know could only lead you further into crime? Are you feeling that you need to change your life and do something better?

## MAY NEED HELP MAKING A CHANGE

Well, you can make a change in your life. You have to be serious about wanting change. You also have to be serious about leaving criminal activity behind, if you are already involved in it. Make a clean break, but you may need help to sort through a number of things. If you have a probation officer or a social worker, speak to that person. Maybe you are not yet fully involved in a criminal way of life, but you have been doing things that you know are definitely wrong and could lead you down the wrong path. You should speak to someone about it, probably a counsellor, a social worker, a minister, or maybe a caring adult or a friend.

## PARENTS MAY BE THE BEST HELP

Your parents may get angry at you at times, because you keep doing the same things that get you into trouble each time. However, if your parents were to know that you really needed help in making a change, and that you are serious and committed about this, they would very likely be your staunchest supporters. They want good things for you and they become frustrated when they see you sabotaging your future. Talking things out usually helps in putting ideas and feelings into perspective. You may talk to an older adult, a grandparent, or someone you know as a responsible adult. These individuals could also put you in contact with resources that would help you straighten out your life, pursue further education, and become a self-supporting individual.

## BE SELF-AWARE

As pointed out earlier, emotional intelligence involves being self-aware. Recognize when you may not be doing the right things and when you need to make a change in your life. But you may think that things have gone badly for so long that maybe it does not make sense trying to change.

Knowing that all things are possible if you believe, tell yourself "I can do it!" Remember, you are the only person that could make the right change in your life. If you do not take action, nothing will change.

If you take action by breaking with the past, by leaving any criminal activity behind, and tell yourself consistently that you can do it, you will come to believe it, especially as you see change starting to happen.

Maybe you are not caught up in any such activity, but you can still be self-aware, recognizing that the positive things that you do can only help you to be a better person.

## CHAPTER 5: *REFERENCES AND FURTHER READING -*

Carlo, Gustavo, Marcela Raffaelli, Deborah J. Laible and Kathryn A. Meyer, "Why are girls less physically aggressive than boys? Personality and parental mediators of physical aggression," *Sex Roles*, May 1999, 40 (9/10).

Gilligan, J. (2010). Men's Voices, Men as Allies: Excerpt from Violence: Reflections on a National Epidemic. Available at http://www.feminist.com/resources/artspeech/mensvoices17.html

Ronk, M.J., Hund, A.M., & Landau, S. (2011). Assessment of social competence of boys with attention-deficit/hyperactivity disorder: Problematic peer entry, host responses, and evaluations. *Journal of Abnormal Child Psychology, 39*, 829-840.

# CHAPTER 6

# STRESS AND EMOTIONS

## STRESS: WHO NEEDS IT?

### EVERYONE AND NO ONE

What does stress mean to you? Is it motivating or debilitating?

Everyone needs a certain level of stress to get going, and to be able to adjust well to his or her circumstances. According to Hans Selye, the definitive expert on stress, everyone needs 'eustress' or good stress. Eustress occurs when there is a change in our environment that teaches us to cope in a better way with situations in our lives. Other than this, no one needs stress.

### WHAT IS STRESS?

The word 'stress' implies that there is a great deal of pressure being applied to the individual, and this could take many forms. For adults, it could be work-related. For young people, it could be school-related. It could also be based on relationships that are not going well, or on feelings of uncertainty or dissatisfaction about particular situations. Stress could also come about because of money problems. Some young people experience stress because of how they look, or how they think other people see them. Stress therefore represents the response of the individual to his or her environment as he or she tries to cope with varying situations.

## RESPONSE TO STRESS

It is well-known that there are two responses to stress: fight or flight. What happens to our emotions during stress? When individuals feel in control of their situation, they often do not experience stress. Stress often arises when they feel that they are not in control of a particular situation or in control of their lives.

## EMOTIONAL SYMPTOMS OF STRESS

Some of the symptoms of stress that one can look out for are moodiness, irritability or short-temperedness, feelings of agitation and inability to relax, feeling overwhelmed, and feeling generally unhappy and depressed. It is also possible to have a strong feeling of loneliness and of being isolated.

## CAUSES OF STRESS: EXTERNAL

In some instances, individuals undergo stress because of things that are happening in their lives. These could be life changes, changes in circumstances, or stressful global events. Adolescents experience more situations that cause them stress, with some of the most commonly reported one having to do with interpersonal relationships, and these could include conflicts with parents, siblings, peers, and boy/girlfriends (Williamson et al, 2003; Anderson, Salk, & Hyde, 2015). At the same time, some of these same relationships can help in dealing with other stressful situations (Anderson et al., 2015).

## LIFE CHANGES

These may be life changes such as a move to a new city, death of a loved one, or illnesses. Many individuals find it very stressful moving to a new city to live, because they have to re-create the life that they left behind. This may mean forming new friendships and just getting to know where things are. In other words, they have to change their routines and create new ones. For children and young people, stress could involve divorce and having a new set of living conditions.

## CHANGES IN CIRCUMSTANCES

Some people experience stress because of lack of a job, money, or opportunity. Maybe stress comes in the form of not being able to meet one's financial obligations. Some individuals may remain in the same place, but they find that their circumstances change. For children and young people, it could be that they have a new teacher, do not understand the class work that they are being taught, and they may be fearful of failing, or even of not graduating.

## STRESSFUL EVENTS IN SOCIETY

"No man is an island" is a line of the British poet, John Donne, and clearly explains what happens when there are stressful situations in our society. We are all affected, when we hear of disaster that has befallen someone. A catastrophic car accident, an airline crash, the devastation that has resulted from a hurricane or tornado, the shooting of a young man, the massacre at a theatre, and the collapse of a roller coaster are all events that affect us greatly, even though we may not be aware of the extent. However, although we may not be directly involved, and we may not have family members or friends involved, we still may become sad or distraught by the very fact that these events have taken place. They have affected our human condition.

## CAUSES OF STRESS: INTERNAL

But there are also internal factors that can contribute to stress. For example, some people just worry a great deal about most things in their lives. Some individuals are naturally pessimists, as they see most things going bad, even when things are going well.

## CHILDREN AND YOUNG PEOPLE HAVE STRESS, TOO

When we think of stress, we usually think of adults, and only distantly about children and young people. The truth is that adults, young people and children suffer from stress, and while stress in adults is usually addressed, that of children and young people is often ignored, and often thought of as being non-existent or not being serious.

A parent, speaking about her teenage son, asked rhetorically: "What does he have to stress him out?" My thought was: "More than you can think!" Young people have a great deal of stress from numerous sources, and additional stress comes from not being able to control situations, and from not having this stress recognized. Even when there are no specific changes in circumstances, young people experience stress because of their particular life cycle.

## STRESS AND YOUNG PEOPLE – PLACE OF GOALS

One of the main reasons for stress at this age is that young people may have self-concerns. Many young people worry whether they are able to meet personal goals, goals that their parents may have set for them, or even goals that they may have set for themselves earlier. If these goals are too high, many young people see themselves as failing. On the other hand, if goals are too low, some young people also experience stress, for they may feel that they are not doing as much for themselves as they should, and that there is no challenge. Some young people experience stress that is associated with low self-esteem and lack of confidence in their abilities; or they may be grappling with their sexual identity, particularly if they believe that they may appear different from other people in some way.

## FAMILY SITUATIONS

Some young people may experience stress over home conditions and their particular family situations. They may experience stress in the home when parents make too many demands, when the family is in crisis, or when they feel that they are not being given the attention that they need. Stress could arise when young people feel they cannot cope. Some experts identify severe marital problems and abuse, overcrowding, low social status, criminality or psychiatric disorders in parents, or a combination of these, as factors that cause stress in young people.

## SCHOOL

Some young people feel stress over school. They may be anxious about how teachers and other students would relate or are relating to them. Some young people experience stress because they find the curriculum boring, or because they are disinterested in school. Some feel stress because others tease or bully them. The level of noise in a class, the way a teacher corrects a student's behavior or the pressure put on young people to perform may also contribute to stress. There is also stress that comes from failing subjects, and from the low self-esteem that is associated with the feeling of being a failure. Some young people feel stress when they have to do tests or exams.

## COMPETITION

Added to this, there could be stress from competition with other young people, and this is as much a problem in the classroom as at home. When teachers or parents compare students or siblings with each other, those that are not doing very well often feel stress. Some young people often feel stress when they have to be taken out of their regular class and put into a special class. It is believed that young people who are singled out and made to feel that they are not as bright or as good as the others often experience stress because of this.

## ROLE OF TRAUMA

Many young people experience traumatic incidents in their lives. Many of these experiences remain imprinted on the minds of these young people, and may be a constant reminder of the incidents. This may also lead to mental problems in childhood, adolescence, as well as later in life.

## MEDICAL PROBLEMS

Young people who have medical problems often experience stress over their condition. Part of the reason may be that they feel ill or that they cannot participate in the activities that they would normally engage in if they were not ill. Another may be the fact that the illness is very serious and life-threatening.

## PHYSICAL DISABILITIES

Young people who have physical disabilities and who are aware of these often experience stress. They may see themselves as not being able to do what others can. In some cases, a young person may see a physical feature as a disability, when such a feature may not even catch the attention of others. Nevertheless, it may be still a source of stress to a young person.

## DIFFERENCE

Many young people experience stress because they are different from others, and they are made to feel that way. One of the major causes of difference is that of race or ethnicity, and for children and young people who do not have a strong sense of pride in who they are, this could be stressful, when they see themselves as different from others, or when they are made to feel different (Chandra & Batala, 2006).

## GREATER AWARENESS NEEDED

What this reveals is that some young people may have more sources of stress than their parents or adults in general. Yet, because it is often thought that young people are too young to have stress, it is overlooked to the detriment of the young person. It is important that parents, teachers, and adults interacting with children and young people be aware of the prevalence of stress at this age.

## CONDITIONS THAT NEED ATTENTION

While some of these stresses may disappear over a short period of time, some are more long-standing. When these stresses become so severe that they affect our daily living, make us less productive, and may even lead to depression, it is time to seek out some counselling.

Counselling does not mean that you have to go into any long-term process, but sometimes, it makes sense to speak to someone else about these feelings. This is particularly important for teens and young adults, and this is why when there are traumatic situations taking place in their environment, for example, when a classmate is shot or when there is violence in a work setting, counsellors are often provided. In younger age groups, as when a classmate dies, many teachers may also have a discussion with the children about the event that may have happened. In other words, it is important to process difficult situations, so that there is an understanding of what has happened. This is an excellent practice, regardless of the age of the young person that may be affected.

## COULD BE A MOTIVATING FACTOR

On the other hand, there are many young people who have all or some of these sources of stress, and who do not succumb to them. Some explanation for this can be found in a pilot study by Romeo (2014), in which this research identified factors that accounted in part for the resilience of some adolescents to stress. Some of the possible factors identified were genetic, sex/gender differences, early life programming of the hypothalamic-pituitary-adrenal (GPA) axis, and inoculation to stress as a result of early exposure to some stress (Romeo, 2014). It is also possible that some young people have learned how to use coping mechanisms to reduce the effect of stress.

If you are one of these young people, you must be thankful for your resilience in being able to deal with stress. Whenever possible, use coping mechanisms that help you to cope with difficult situations. However, many, in fact, use stress as a motivating, rather than as a debilitating, influence on their lives.

## LOOK FOR HELP

However, if you are a young person who is experiencing a great deal of stress, and this stress is having a debilitating effect on you, you need to look for help. Stress is something that could take a severe toll on you mentally, emotionally, and physically. It can also take a severe toll on your health. Therefore, if you are experiencing a great deal of stress, or maybe you just feel continuously depressed, a good idea is to discuss it with an adult, parent, teacher, social worker, or your family doctor, since stress could erode your mental health and other systems. By taking action to address your source(s) of stress, you will be taking an important step in alleviating it and protecting your mental health.

# CHAPTER 6 - REFERENCES AND FURTHER READING

Anderson, S. F., Salk, R. H. & Hyde, J. S. (2015). Stress in romantic relationships and adolescent depressive symptoms: Influence of parental support. *Journal of Family Psychology, 29*(3), 339-348.

Bratsis, M. E. (2012). The stress response: The good and the bad. *The Science Teacher,* 79(9). 74.

Bryant, S. E. & Malone, T. I. (2015). An empirical study of emotional Intelligence and stress in college students. *Business Education and Accreditation,* 7(1), 1-12.

Chandra, A. & Batada, A. (2006). Exploring stress and coping among urban African American Adolescents: The Shifting the Lens study. *Preventing Chronic Disease, 3*(2), A40.

Field, T., Diego, M. & Sanders, C. (2001). Adolescent depression and risk factors. *Adolescence,* 36(143), 491-498.

Griffith, M. A., Dubow, E. F. & Ippoloto, M. F. (2000). Developmental and

Cross-Situational Differences in Adolescents' Coping Strategies," *Journal of Youth and Adolescence,* 29(2), 183-204.

Pace, B. (2000). Helping Children Cope with Violence. *The Journal of the American Medical Association,* 284(5). 654.

Romeo, R. D. (2014). Perspectives on stress resilience and adolescent neurobehavioral function. *Neurobiology of Stress, 1,* 128-133.

Tovar-Murray, D. & Munley, P. H. (2007). Exploring the relationship between race-related stress, identity, and well-being among African Americans. *The Western Journal of Black Studies, 31*(1), 58-70.

Turaga, R. (2016). On Managing Emotions. *IUP Journal of Soft Skills, 10* (1), 16-25.

Williamson, D. E., Birmaher, B., Ryan, N.D., Shiffrin, T. P., Lusky, J.A. et al. (2003). The stressful life events schedule for children and adolescents: Development and validation. *Psychiatry Research, 119*, 225-241.

# CHAPTER 7

# HOW STRESS AFFECTS EMOTIONS

Do you sometimes feel like staying by yourself and not speaking to anyone? Do you sometimes feel 'blue' and am not sure why you feel this way? Do you sometimes feel out of sorts and feel like avoiding everyone, including your family members? There could be several reasons for this, but is it likely that you are dealing with some stress? It's worth it to try to explore why you feel this way, why your emotions seem to be out of balance.

Many young people are thought to be acting out or to be going through a phase, when they experience stress. Many adults take it that in time the young person would 'snap out' of whatever is bothering him or her, or whatever is causing the young person to act irrationally at times. In some cases, this happens and the young person starts acting rationally again.

## GIVING IT SOME THOUGHT

It could be that the young person may have been just a little depressed about himself, how he looks, and what his friends may be thinking about it. After thinking, he has come to accept his uneven growth, his awkwardness, or any of the idiosyncrasies that come with maturing.

Or the young person may have been concerned that she does not have many friends, that certain of the girls are avoiding her, and she feels left out. After thinking for some time, she may come to accept that things are what they are.

# YOUNGSTERS MAY NEED HELP DEALING WITH STRESS

But sometimes, young people do not get over these feelings so easily.

In many instances, young people need some help in working things out. Sometimes, they need to discuss certain concerns they may have, especially when they feel that there is no one that would listen, understand or even believe them. Sometimes, a young person needs to be able to sort things out for himself or herself.

## FIND SOMEONE TO TALK

If you are a young person with something bothering you, it is best to find someone with whom you could discuss it. You would be surprised at the number of adults or other young people who have gone through the same difficulties that you may be going through now, or who had the same concerns that you are experiencing. You may find out that what you thought was unique to you is something that many people are concerned about as well.

## DON'T KEEP STRESS BOTTLED UP

You may also be upset with someone or with some situation. Rather than talk about it in an effort to change things, you may decide to keep quiet about it. This does not help the situation, because nothing has changed for the better. In fact, things could become worse, because you may be getting angrier with the person or the situation. You may even find that your anger has gone out of control. You may find that you are having inappropriate outbursts, and that you sometimes become irrational. You may even start thinking of revenge. This is dangerous. Talk to someone.

## ASK FOR HELP

It is time to find help. There is nothing wrong with feeling lost, or with not being able to cope. Many people go through this on a daily basis. The difference between learning to cope and staying lost is that some people ask for help and others do not.

## IT'S GOOD MENTAL HEALTH

Besides, there is the larger picture of stress brought on by unfortunate events on a global scale. It is not unusual for young people, like children and adults, to feel unsafe because of these events. However, young people who feel a loss of control over their lives, who feel anxious, or who may have intense and confused feelings because of everything that is taking place around them should speak to their parents, their friends, and/or seek professional help. This is important for maintaining good mental health.

## ESPECIALLY CHILDREN

As Steven Marans, associate professor of child psychoanalysis and psychiatry, and director of the National Center for Children Exposed to Violence (at Yale University School of Medicine), points out: "When children who have been affected by catastrophic events are left unattended, they are also left emotionally dislocated and mute. Like adult survivors, traumatized children may also need help finding a voice that not only captures the pain, fear, and outrage that is shared, but that reflects the courage required to speak to them as well" (Marans, 2004).

It is therefore important that young people who may have experienced these emotions in childhood and who are feeling its effects in adolescence, discuss their feelings with their parents, as well as a professional. In doing this, a young person would be taking measures to protect his or her mental health.

## THERE IS ALWAYS HELP AVAILABLE SOMEWHERE

Regardless of the source of stress, it could be helped. If you are failing at school, you could seek tutoring. You could seek a professional outside of school, but you may find that you could get help from your teachers, from friends, and from family members.

## PARENTS AND OTHERS COULD HELP

Do not underestimate the amount of help your parents can give. If your stress persists, you may want to speak to your parents, as well as seek out a professional, for example, your school social worker, a child and youth worker, or your guidance counsellor at school. You may also seek help from your family doctor or from a walk-in clinic or a mental health clinic. All of these professionals would be happy to help you organize your affairs, help you get back on track, and help you deal with anxieties that may be affecting your mental health. When you get help, make use of the resources that are provided for you.

## PROTECT YOUR MENTAL HEALTH AT ALL TIMES

Remember, we all need to talk things out with others from time to time, and there is no weakness in asking for help when we begin to feel overwhelmed by life's circumstances. If there is something that is causing you worry, deal with it. If you feel stress over certain situations, try to resolve what is causing you stress. Realize that stress can take a toll on your mental health. Therefore, it is a healthy approach to be proactive in dealing with our mental health.

## CHAPTER 7 - *REFERENCES AND FURTHER READING*

Marans, S. (2005). When We All Need Someone to Lean On. *International Journal of Group Psychotherapy*, 55(3), 43-54.

Pace, B. (2000). Helping Children Cope with Violence. *The Journal of the American Medical Association*, 284(5), 654

Turaga, R. (2016). On Managing Emotions. IUP Journal of Soft Skills, Vol. 10(1), 16-25.

Webb, N. B (2004). Mass Trauma and Violence: Helping Families and Children Cope. New York: Guilford Press.

# CHAPTER 8

# TALKING YOURSELF INTO A STRESSFUL SITUATION

Do you ever find that you are talking yourself into a stressful situation? Nothing is wrong, but you are imagining situations that could occur and you end up being stressful about what isn't?

Some individuals sabotage their own success. Although things may be going well, they continue to convince themselves that this is not the case. The result is that they talk themselves into feeling badly about themselves. What has actually happened in a case such as this is that the person has self-generated the stress that afflicts him or her.

## PERFECTIONISM AND UNREALISTIC EXPECTATIONS

Trying to accomplish unrealistic goals could be very stressful, as the individuals are forever striving for perfection which continues to elude them. This could be very frustrating to these individuals and could actually slow them down in achieving any goals. At the same time, while you can use "what if" scenarios to develop goals, do not use "what ifs" as excuses that prevent you from achieving your goals. As David (May 29, 2012) advises that according to research, "[w]hen you ponder what could have gone better, or recognize obstacles in your way, you generate valuable information. Identify factors within your control, and see what you can do about them." In other words, you look for the opportunities where you can exercise control.

## TAKING AN ALL-OR-NOTHING ATTITUDE

Some individuals take the position that they would either do something well or not do it at all While this could be motivational in helping an individual to put his or her best foot forward, it can also be detrimental. With this attitude, an individual may feel defeated if he or she feels inadequate to achieve a certain goal, and therefore gives up the option to try, to make an error, and to try again. This could also be a source much stress. Taking the attitude of trying until one is successful is often a way to relieve this kind of stress.

## FAMILY STRESS

Sometimes stress comes about because of difficulties in relationships. Infidelity towards one's partner, or infidelity on the part of one's partner, either cheating or being cheated on, could be a major source of stress for many young people. However, sometimes there is nothing happening, but by imagining that it could happen, one thinks that it is happening, and so creates a stressful situation that does not exist. The result could be conflict in relationships that need not have occurred.

## BEING TOO BUSY

Being too busy can be a source of stress, for some individuals find that they are unable to keep track of the many activities for which they are responsible. In many cases, the stress is self-inflicted, as some individuals often take on more than they are able to handle. In other words, they overcommit themselves, and find out too late that they are unable to handle their responsibilities appropriately. Yet, they struggle to keep up, being too busy to attend to the things that are personal to them: their family commitments. This is self-inflicted stress.

## WHEN STRESS LEADS TO VIOLENCE

Sometimes, when individuals find their stress unbearable, they can become despondent, angry or depressed. These emotions can be sometimes associated with violence, if individuals feel that others have contributed to the level of stress they are experiencing. It is important to recognize when your stress is leading you to carry out violence or to even think about it. At this point, you need to take a step back and consider how your emotions have become so intense that you are becoming irrational.

## CHAPTER 8: *REFERENCES AND FURTHER READING*

David, S. (May 29, 2012). Don't sabotage yourself. *Harvard Business Review.* Retrieved from https://hbr.org/2012/05/dont-sabotage-yourself

Houltberg, B. J., Henry, B. J., Morris, C. S., & Sheffield, A. (2012). Family interactions, exposure to violence and emotional regulation: Perceptions of children and early adolescents at risk. *Family Relations, 61*(2), 283-296.

Sharma, S. (2014). Exposure to community violence: Post traumatic stress disorder symptoms, impairment functioning and achievement motivation among Grade 8th and 10th adolescents. *International Journal of Education and Management Studies, 4*(4), 1-10.

# CHAPTER 9

# GETTING YOUR EMOTIONS UNDER CONTROL

Researchers have shown that individuals exhibit several negative emotions when they are under stress. While it is important to eliminate the source of stress, this is not always easy to do. Recognizing that your stress is responsible for your emotional state and the symptoms you display is the first step in trying to control how you express your emotions.

## THINGS TO DO TO MANAGE STRESS

Talk and socialize with family members, provided that family members are not the source of your stress. Meet with friends for coffee or dinner. Tap into your support system, do physical exercise, and don't over-indulge in food.

## TAP INTO YOUR SUPPORT SYSTEM

Tap into your support system, namely family members and friends. Some young people also have a mentor that they could turn to when they are experiencing a great deal of stress. At times, it may be necessary to speak to a school counsellor. This allows for social engagement which is important to help you not to feel isolated. For those without family and friends around, it may be helpful to try and join a club or other organization where it is possible to develop personal relations with others.

## PHYSICAL HEALTH/MENTAL HEALTH

Another way to manage stress is to try to improve your physical health. If you are physically well, you are more likely to feel good or at least better about yourself. Taking up an exercise routine may also help you feel better. Doing it in a gym setting with other people may even be better.

## MOOD AND FOOD

Another way of managing stress is to look at what you eat. Food can have a profound effect on mood. This is why some people speak about comfort foods. While having a good meal you enjoy may improve your mood, don't overdo it. Eat wisely and follow good nutritional practices.

## FEELING IN CONTROL

A fourth way of managing stress is to promote mastery. Finding areas where you have control and where you excel is important. If you feel that you excel at what you do, you are more likely to have a stronger sense of self. Taking up a hobby and spending time to excel it can be a very helpful way to feel in control.

## CONTROLLING YOUR EMOTIONS

A fifth way of managing stress is knowing how to control your emotions. When you get angry, think of something that you can change your emotions. You may have an activity that causes you to calm down.

## CHECK IMPULSIVITY

One important point to bear in mind when dealing with your emotions is to never do anything impulsively. Always stop and count to 10 before acting. This will give you time to think and it will very likely prevent you from saying or doing something that you may regret.

## KNOW THE NATURE OF YOUR STRESS

When faced with a stressful situation, it is best to find out as much as possible about the nature of the situation. Try to control elements of the situation so that you can know what to expect. Eliminating sources of uncertainty would help you expect what is coming. You would be very likely under less stress.

## RELAXATION IS KEY

Researchers tells us to find a way to relax. Some people use meditation, for example, yoga, where they could relax their minds and their bodies. Other people spend time praying and reading the Bible or other religious text. A major consideration is to spend time reflecting and clearing one's minds of negative thoughts by reading materials that stress positive outlook on life.

## SLEEP TO MANAGE STRESS

When you are sleepy, you are likely to be irritable and experience greater stress. By sleeping adequately at night, you can feel under less stress the following day. People who work night shift are very prone to experience greater stress than those who work regular hours.

## CUT BACK ON CAFFEINE

Cut back on caffeine as much as possible. This means cutting back on coffee and tea, and using instead fresh fruit and vegetables. Having a good breakfast without caffeine also helps.

## IDENTIFY SOURCES OF STRESS AND HOW THEY AFFECT EMOTIONS

This will help you explain why you feel the way you do at times. This will also help you decide how to alleviate your stress in the future.

## KNOW YOUR BODY AND STRESS

Recognize how your body responds to stress, particularly how you feel emotionally when you experience stress. For example, you may not be able to sleep, may well experience depression, low energy and low motivation. Some people experience headaches, stomach aches, palpitation of the heart, cold sweat, or trembling of the hands (Mayo Clinic, 2017). These are only some of the symptoms that people experience. Know what you feel and how to deal with these. If you recognize how your body responds to the different sources of stress, you will be better able to know how to deal with the various symptoms of stress, and therefore be better able to manage them.

## MUSIC CALMS THE SPIRIT

Music is recognized as an important means of dealing with stress. Over the years, everyday people as well as studies have shown that when people to music, it has a calming effect on them. Studies have shown that when individuals listen to music that stress has of an impact on them (Thoma, La Marca, Bronnimann, Finkel, Ehlert & Nater, 2013).

Listening to music can therefore have a calming effect on individuals, either before a stressful situation or after. You have probably found this out for yourself, and know that when you listen to your music, you feel more at ease with the difficult situations you may be going through.

## CHAPTER 9: *REFERENCES AND FURTHER READING*

American Psychological Association (2017). Teens and stress: How to keep stress in check. Retrieved from *http://www.apa.org/helpcenter/stress-teens.aspx*

Byrne, D. G., Davenport, S. C., & Mazanov, J. (2007). Profiles of adolescent stress: The development of the adolescent stress questionnaire. *Journal of Adolescence, 30,* 393-416.

Goodman, E., McEwen, B. S., Dolan, L. M., Schafer-Kalkhoff, T. & Adler, N. E. (2005). Social disadvantage and adolescent stress. *Journal of Adolescent Health,* 37, 484-492.

Guszkowska, M. (2005). Physical fitness as a resource in coping with stress among high school students. Journal of Sports Medicine and Physical Fitness, 45, 105-111.

Kadapatti, M. C. & Vijayalaxmi, A. (2012). Stressors of academic stress: A study of pre-university students. *Indian Journal of Scientific Research, 3,* 171-175.

Mayo Clinic (2017). Stress symptoms: Effects on your body and behavior. Retrieved from http://www.mayoclinic.org/healthy-lifestyle/stress-management/in-depth/stress-symptoms/art-20050987

Thoma, M. V., LaMarca, R., Bronnimann, R., Finkel, L., Ehlert, U. & Nater, U. M. (2013). The effect of music on the human stress response. *PLOS ONE, 8*(8), 1-12

CHAPTER 10

# USING EMOTIONAL INTELLIGENCE IN THE WORKPLACE

Research has shown that emotional intelligence plays an important role in the workplace as it leads to greater efficiency and success for the workplace and to a better experience for the workers. One of the most common problems pertaining to emotional intelligence in the workplace is bullying. What is needed in the case of the workplace where employees are bullied is greater emotional management.   This will come about if an employer recognizes that by managing his or her emotions at work that he or she can possibly change the environment. Or if a workplace bully realizes the toll he or she is having on co-workers, and on the workplace as a whole, the bully may decide to change his or her ways.

## NATURE OF EMOTIONAL INTELLIGENCE

As noted earlier, emotional intelligence involves the dimensions of self-awareness, managing one's emotions, self-motivation, and developing effective communication skills.  By becoming self-aware, recognizing one's emotions in the workplace, one can strive to manage one's emotions so as to display appropriate behavior in dealing with others.

## MANAGING YOUR EMOTIONS

One of the ways of managing your emotions is to strive to influence how other people respond to you. Researchers claim that by sharing how you feel and by cooperating and connecting with others, you will feel more comfortable with others and would developed greater trust with co-workers. Co-workers would very likely then feel comfortable sharing their emotions with you. In a workplace, this could be advantageous, as there could be less confusion over each other's behavior.

## REDUCING VICTIMIZATION WITH EMOTIONAL INTELLIGENCE

It is by working to develop your emotional intelligence that you could strive to reduce the victimization or bullying that takes place in the workplace. In some cases, people who bully others may only be concerned with how the bullying makes them feel, and may not give thought to the feelings of the person who is being bullied. By expressing your feelings, it is possible to have an effect on those who are bullies. It does not always happen this way, as some bullies are well aware of the possible effects their bullying can cause, and intend to have these effects.

## ORGANIZATIONS NEED TO TAKE ACTION

The organization where bullying takes place needs to take action to reduce this practice. One of the ways to doing this is to take action to build trust among employees. If employees trust their organization, they will be more likely to trust others in the organization and be more ready to open up to each other. If employees believe that their organization can be trusted to be just and fair, then they would be more willing to discuss bullying that they are experiencing in the organization. If the employees do not trust the organization, then many of them would be more likely to leave the organization. Employees are also more ready to deal with changes in the organization when they have greater organizational trust.

## EFFECTIVE LEADERS ARE EMOTIONALLY INTELLIGENT

Effective leaders in organizations must have good self-awareness and understand the importance of self-management or managing their emotions. This will lead to their better treatment of their employees and less stress in their departments.

### BOSSY LEADERS OFTEN LOSE

Leaders who tend to be very bossy and not aware of their effect on their employees often end up not having a very efficiently run department or company. They often have tension-filled work environments, where absenteeism is frequent and employee turnover is high.

### YOUR CHOICE AS MANAGER

If you are a manager in one of these settings, and do not really understand why your department is in such a state of tension, where turnover is unacceptably high, start looking closely at how you behave, and how you treat your employees. Ask yourself, "How do my employees see me?" Put yourself in your employees' shoes and ask yourself how you would have felt if you were an employee in your department. You may find that you do not really take your employees' feelings into consideration.

## START MANAGING YOUR EMOTIONS

Start managing your emotions, and treating your employees the way you would want to be treated. Realize that you have a choice. You could continue being the manager who is a bully to your employees, who may overlook the bullying that is taking place in your workplace, or who may be creating an intolerable condition in your department because you are not self-aware. Or you can take stock of what is happening in your department, ask yourself what role your behavior towards your employees has in creating the environment. If you still do not know what is causing your employees so much stress and why they are leaving, try to find out from them. Ask them. However, give them the opportunity to provide you with information anonymously. If your employees do not trust you, or the organization, they may be afraid of losing their jobs if they tell you directly what is wrong. Give them the opportunity to be candid without disclosing their identity.

## CHAPTER 10: *REFERENCES AND FURTHER READING*

Ashraf, F. & Khan, M. A. (2014). Does emotional intelligence moderate the relationship between workplace bullying and job performance? *Asian Business & Management, 13*(2), 171-190.

Brotheridge, C. M. & Lee, R. T. (2010). Restless and confused: Emotional responses to workplace bullying in men and women. *Career Development International, 15*(7), 687-707.

Kannaiah, D. & Shanthi, R. (2015). A study on emotional intelligence at work place. European Journal of Business and Management, 7(24), 147-154.

Mathisen, G. E., Einarsen, S., & Reidar, M. (2011). The relationship between supervisor, personality, and supervisor's perceived stress and workplace bullying. *Journal of Business Ethics, 99*(4), 637-651.

Zeidner, M., Matthews, G. & Roberts, R. D. (2004). Emotional intelligence in the workplace: A critical review. *International Association for Applied Psychology, 53*(3), 371-399.

# CHAPTER 11

# MANAGING YOUR EMOTIONS IN THE WORKPLACE

## DEALING WITH BULLYING

Some may think of workplaces as devoid of emotions, especially when management has specific rules against romantic relations between employees. However, emotions appear in workplaces in many different ways, one of which is through bullying. In many workplaces, young workers, and older ones too, encounter bullying. The type of bullying that occurs in the workplace may differ from that which takes place in the classroom, but may be just as oppressive.

## FORMS OF BULLYING IN THE WORKPLACE

Bullying in the workplace could involve criticism of an employee's work, the manner of speech used to address the employee, the kinds of jobs that are given to certain employees in the workplace, and imitation of the manner in which an employee speaks or of the employee's accent. Or bullying could be indirect reference to an employee's way of working. In short, bullying could take the form of any behavior that makes an employee feel poorly about himself or herself. Bullying could also involve an employee being left out of a social grouping in the department or unit, so that the employee that is being bullied feel ostracized. At times, bullying in the workplace could involve pressure being placed on an employee by a manager or supervisor of the department, in an effort to get more work done.

## BULLYING IS A FORM OF VIOLENCE AND VICTIMIZATION

Bullying is a form of violence, where individuals are victimized. Bullying in organizations destroy individuals as well as organizations. Usually in an organizational setting, bullying involves insulting, humiliating, abusing, intimidating, and displaying offensive and often malicious behavior (Rhodes, Pullen, Vickers, Clegg & Pitsis, 2010).

## CONSEQUENCES OF BULLYING FOR THE WORKER

An employee may experience a great amount of stress as a result of working in an environment where he or she may be bullied. This has consequences for the employee. As one author points out, "Stress-causing work conditions create pressure and difficulty for employees and create anxiety" (Oktug, 2013, p. 82). Bullying in the workplace increases negative moods and decreases positive feelings, reduces job satisfaction, and leads to depression, and lack of organizational commitment. Some groups can experience bullying because of their demographic status. As Okechukwu (2014) points out, "Members of demographic minority groups are more likely to be victims of workplace injustice and suffer more adverse outcomes when exposed to workplace injustice compared to demographic majority groups" (p. 573). This can have severe consequences for those that are bullied, for example, those that impact their health. Many people who are bullied experience severe depression and other ills (Okechukwu, 2014).

# CONSEQUENCES OF BULLYING FOR THE ORGANIZATION

There are also consequences for the workplace, as workers who are bullied tend to be less productive, with the work place experiencing greater absenteeism and more employee turnover. As Ashraf and Khan (2014) maintain, the negative impacts on an organization are decreased work satisfaction on the part of employees, increased turnover, lack of morale and poor organizational performance.

## HIGH EMOTIONAL INTELLIGENCE AS ANTIDOTE

Although some employees are bullied and choose to leave an organization, some may remain in the setting. In fact, research has shown that although bullying has a negative impact on job performance, sometimes employees with high emotional intelligence could experience less of a negative impact on job performance. In this case, it is the high emotional intelligence that has moderated the negative impact.

## MANAGERS SHOULD KNOW BETTER

Managers may sometimes use bullying in order to get results and reach organizational goals (Ashraf & Khan, 2014). Sometimes a manager may be hostile to an employee or even make inappropriate jokes in order to defuse stress, but this could be perceived by the employees as unsatisfactory or even abusive behavior. It is whatever the employer or manager does and what the employee may see as bullying that gets called by that name (Ashraf & Khan, 2014). Managers within these organizations must recognize these relationships. Managers should know better, and should do something when they see bullying taking place on their watch.

## BULLYING BY COWORKERS

Some employees are bullied by their co-workers when they go against the decisions of these co-workers. For example, if workers decide to do only a certain amount of work per day and one employee decides to work at peak performance, that employee could be ostracized. On the other hand, an employee could be bullied if other workers see him or her as a threat.

## BULLYING BY ORGANIZATIONS

Usually, it is individuals within organizations that carry out the bullying, but there are organizations that also have systems in place that bully their employees. For example, there are some organizations that dictate the amount of work that must be done, and employees who do not achieve the volume of work prescribed can be threatened or even dismissed.

## BULLYING BY MANAGERS

Managers may bully their employees, if they believe they could get more performance and work out of the employee. Some managers, in order to compete with other managers, try to show that their departments are more productive. These managers may put more pressure on workers to produce or to work at certain times (Ashraf & Khan, 2014).

## MANAGERS BLAMING THE ORGANIZATIONS FOR BULLYING

Some managers take the position that they cannot be responsible for the systems within the organizations for which they work, but many employees hold managers personally responsible and so target managers with their anger and violence. Employees can feel bullied when they are forced to work long hours and often without pay. Some employees feel bullied when they cannot choose the hours of their work or when they cannot decide on when to take vacation.

## AN EXAMPLE OF ORGANIZATIONAL BULLYING

According to its employees, one large box store, while paying their employees lower wages that other companies in their sector, prevent their employees from doing part-time work anywhere else. The managers insist that employees be available to work at any time, which means that these workers could be called in on any shift. This prevents these employees from picking up part-time work anywhere else. If a manager calls an employee in to work and that employee refuses to come in, that employee could easily find that he or she may not be scheduled to work for several days, thereby penalizing that employee for not being available when the company wanted him or her to work.

Employees feel bullied by their companies when they are restricted in how they must carry out the work, even when employees realize that this is not the most efficient and humane way of doing the work. This is a good example of how managers and their organizations can bully some of their workers.

## HOW MANAGERS CAN HELP

One way of dealing with employees who are frustrated and disgruntled is for managers to discuss the situation with their employees and their upper management when they realize that the grievances of their employees are justified. Managers, though representing the interests of their companies must also advocate for their employees.

## WHEN MANAGERS FAIL

Sometimes managers know of the unfairness and injustice in their departments and organizations, but allow these to continue. This complacency could only lead to even more confrontation and sometimes to more violence. This does not have to be the case. These conditions of unfairness and injustice could be addressed and could even be resolved. However, the issue is that managers may be afraid that by presenting the interests of their employees to their employers, that they could find that they are without a job.

## BULLYING AND VIOLENCE IN THE WORKPLACE

How many times have we heard or read about an irate employee confronting a manager with violence? Since managers are the face of the organization to employees, they are often on the receiving end of any anger that employees feel towards the organization. Emotions may run high when individuals feel stuck. Some employees feel stuck in a workplace because they need the work to survive, but the work may be humiliating and low paying, and they may find that they are being bullied. Feeling helpless, angry, and frustrated, some employees lash out against their managers. Some even resort to violence, which is a losing strategy as these employees may end up in court, ultimately in jail, or worse.

## WHAT BULLIED EMPLOYEES CAN DO

If you are an employee and you cannot resolve the problem either with your immediate supervisor or upper management, the best solution may be to find other employment. It is useless using violence against your supervisor and co-workers, because even though they may be hurt, you will have to face the consequences. Violence serves no one's cause. Leaving a job where you are being bullied could only free you up to find a better job and have greater satisfaction. Also, you may find that the company that is allowing an atmosphere of bullying to exist is not really a progressive company, looking out for the interests of its employees.

## SPEAK TO EMPLOYERS, IF MANAGERS ARE NOT HELPING

However, dealing with the issue through the law may be an alternative, and may be approach that will not only solve the problem for you, but that may also make the way easier for other employees to come. Depending on the nature of the bullying, there are different ways to approach it.

## USING THE LAW MUST BE THE LAST RESORT

However, making an attempt to address your employers on the nature of bullying that you are experiencing may be a good first line of approach that could yield good results. It is when this approach does not bring the expected results that employees should look within the law for the best strategy to follow.

## CHAPTER 11: *REFERENCES AND FURTHER READING*

Ashraf, F. & Khan, M. A. (2014). Does emotional intelligence moderate the relationship between workplace bullying and job performance? *Asian Business & Management, 13*(2), 171-190.

Besag, V. E. (2006). Understanding girls' friendships, fights and feuds: A practical approach to girls' bullying. Open University Press.

Glaso, L. & Notelaers, G. (2012). Workplace bullying, emotions and outcomes. *Violence & Victims, 27*(3), 360-370

McQuade lll, S.C., Colt, J. P. & Meyer, N. B. B. (2009). Cyber Bullying: Protecting kids and adults from online bullies. Praeger.

Okechukwu, C.A., Souza, K., Davis, K. D. & de Castro, A. B. (2014). Discrimination, harassment, abuse and bullying in the workplace: Contribution of workplace injustice to occupational health disparities. *American Journal of Industrial Medicine, 57*(5), 573-586.

Oktug, Z. (2013). Managing emotions in the workplace: Its mediating effect on the relationship between organizational trust and occupational trust. *International Business Research, 6*(4), 81 – 92.

Rhodes, C., Pullen, A., Vickers, M. H., Clegg, S. R., & Pitsis, A. (2010). Violence and workplace Bullying: what are an organization's ethical responsibilities, *Administrative Theory & Praxis, 32*(1), 96-115

Verkuil, B., Atasayi, S. & Molendijk, M. L. (2015). Workplace bullying and mental health: A meta-analysis on cross-sectional and longitudinal data. *PLOS ONE, 10*(8), 1-16.

CHAPTER 12

# BULLYING AND SELF-HARM:

## MENTAL HEALTH SERVICES NEEDED

Bullying has many serious effects on emotions. Several studies have shown that young people who are bullied often develop serious emotional and psychological disorders. Some of the more common effects are anxiety, depression, sadness, feelings of loneliness, isolation, and a great desire for revenge. Many of these feelings last into adulthood; but they don't have to.

## MORE SERIOUS EFFECTS

Those who are bullied often run the risk of suicide, but bullying may not be the only cause. Many young people who are bullied experience depression as a result of the bullying, but many may also have problems at home, such as divorce and abuse, may have a history of trauma, and may feel different because of sexual orientation, race, or other difference. Many young people who are bullied may also lack support from parents as well as from peers and school officials. But it is possible to get other social support.

## EMOTIONAL COST OF BULLYING

Bullies also experience ill effects. Some may think that bullies are unscathed by the violence because they are the ones that are inflicting the pain on others. However, researchers show that bullies often lack self-confidence, feel badly about themselves, have low self-esteem, feel insecure and even suffer from depression. Both bullies and those that are bullied may also experience mental health problems.

## MENTAL HEALTH COUNSELLING NEEDED

Adolescents who bully and those who are bullied may sometimes engage in self-harm, including cutting and self-battery. These are all serious patterns of behavior that demand immediate mental health attention. These are not the types of behavior that disappear by themselves. Mental health counsellors must be consulted to help deal with any feelings or behaviors that suggest or involve self-harm.

## SOME CAUSES OF SELF-HARM

According to Hay and Meldrum (2010), several recent research studies in the United States reveal that "self-harm is most likely among adolescents who are doing poorly at school, or who have experienced physical or sexual abuse. Additionally, individual characteristics like low self-esteem, impulsivity, and feelings of depression and anxiety contribute to self-harm" (p. 446).

Young people who also have to deal with bullying may also experience these feelings but in greater measure and may see self-harm as their way out of their predicament. But this is not an answer.

## GENERAL STRAIN THEORY AS EXPLANATION

The explanation pertaining to self-harm is that young people experience "strainful social relations" which cause negative emotions, and these negative emotions are associated with self-harm (Hay & Meldrum, 2010, p. 457). Based on these observations, one can use general strain theory to explain why some young people engage in self-harm. Understanding the theory can provide ideas on dealing with this problem.

## IMMEDIATE HELP

Young people who experience any of these feelings need to see out help. Adults,  if you suspect that your young person is having any of these feelings, give them support and help them to find appropriate counselling to deal with these feelings. Don't wait until the situation becomes bad to offer help. When young people are under too much strain, efforts should be made to provide support to offset these negative emotions. It is when young people feel that they are not being heard and experience great distress that they become desperate.  Efforts should be made to help children and adolescents cope with their distress (Fisher et al., 2012).

# CHAPTER 12: *REFERENCES AND FURTHER READING*

Bratsis, M. E. (2013). Preventing bullying at your school. *The Science Teacher, 80*(6), 80-90.

Fisher, H. L., Moffitt, T. E., Houts, R. M., Belsky, D. W., Arseneault, L. & Caspi, A. (2012). Bullying victimization and risk of self-harm in early adolescence: Longitudinal cohort study. *British Medical Journal, 344,* 1-9

Hay, C. & Meldrum, R. (2010). Bully victimization and adolescent self-harm: Hypotheses from General Strain Theory. *Journal of Youth and Adolescence, 39,* 446-459.

Jones, J. R., & Augustine, S. M. (2015). Creating an anti-bullying culture in secondary schools: Characteristics to consider when constructing appropriate anti-bullying programs. *American Secondary Education, 43*(3), 73-83.

Long-term effects of bullying: A notebook of short but worthy items. *Phi Delta Kappan, 94*(8), 6-7

Mirsky, E. L. & Omar, H. A. (2015). Cyberbullying in adolescents: The prevalence of mental disorders and suicidal behavior. *International Journal of Child and Adolescent Health, 8*(1), 37.

Poteat, V. P. P., Rivers, I. & Vecho, O. (2015). The role of peers in predicting students' homophobic behavior: Effects of peer aggression, prejudice and sexual orientation identity importance. *School Psychology Review, 44*(4), 391-406.

Smokowski, P. R., Evans, C. B. & Cotter, K. L. (2014). The differential impacts of episodic, chronic, and cumulative physical bullying and cyberbullying: The effects of victimization on the school experiences, social support and mental health of rural adolescents. *Violence and Victims, 29*(6), 1029-1046.

Xiao, B. S. & Wong, Y. M. (2013). Cyber-bullying among university students: An empirical investigation from the social-cognitive perspective. *International Journal of Business and Information, 8*(1), 34-69.

# TAKING RESPONSIBILITY FOR DEALING WITH BULLYING

When teenagers were questioned about the responsibility for bullying, their answers differ, according to gender. They tended to point to the individual characteristics of the bullies rather than to the peer group, to school setting, or to human nature or society, as reasons.

## BULLYING: WHOSE FAULT – WHAT GIRLS AND BOYS THINK

When girls were asked why bullying takes place, they explained that it is the bully that is more responsible for bullying, while boys pointed out that it is more the victim's fault that bullying occurs. When youth bullies were questioned, they were more likely to say that it was the victim's fault, and less likely to say that it was the bullies themselves that were responsible for the bullying of others (Thornberg & Knutsen, 2011). On the other hand, victims, bystanders, and victim bullies were more likely to say that it was the bully's fault for picking on those to bully (Thornberg & Knutsen, 2011).

# BYSTANDERS NOT IMMUNE – HAVE RESPONSIBILITIES, TOO

Many of those who witness bullying are often fearful to speak up about the bullying they have witnessed, because of fear of retaliation by the bullies. Yet many bystanders believe that what the bully is doing is wrong and may wish to do something about it. Yet, they keep quiet for their own safety.

## BETTER THEM THAN ME

Other bystanders believe that if the bully were to turn his or her attention from the person being bullied that maybe they (the bystanders) may become the new target for the bully. With this thinking, some bystanders believe that by keeping quiet they are keeping themselves from the attention of the bully.

## PEER PRESSURE

Peer pressure also dictates to many bystanders that they should go along with their peers, and do what others around them are doing. Since the bystanders see others around them keeping quiet, they too remain quiet, although they know what is taking place is wrong.

## DIFFERENT EMOTIONS

These different conflicting emotions often take their toll on bystanders, sometimes even to the extent of threatening their mental health. Some bystanders that have not taken a stand against a bully end up feeling so guilty, especially when something tragic happens, that they eventually have to seek out mental health services.

## DOING THE RIGHT THING

If you are a bystander and see someone being bullied, do the right thing and get help for the bully. It is possible that the bully may try turning on you. But remember, if you try to get help, it is likely that you can save the person who is bullied from even more harm.

# CHAPTER 13: REFERENCES AND FURTHER READING

Aldridge, J. (2011). What every teacher should know about bullying. *Childhood Education, 87*(4), 304-306.

Hui, E. K. P., Tsang, S. K. M., & Law, B. C. M. (2012). Combatting school bullying through developmental guidance for positive youth development and promoting harmonious school culture. *International Journal of Child Health and Human development,* 5(1), 2266-2277.

Kalman, I. C. (2013). Why psychology is failing to solve the problem of bullying. *International Journal on World Peace, 30*(2), 71-97.

Swearer, S. M., Turner, R. K., Givens, J. E. & Pollack, W. S. (2008). "You're so gay!" - Do different forms of bullying matter for adolescent males? *School Psychology Review, 37*(2), 160-173.

Thornberg, R. & Knutsen, S. (2011). Teenager' explanation of bullying. *Child and Youth Care Forum, 40,* 177-192.

# CHAPTER 14

# DON'T BE TRAPPED BY DEPRESSION AND VIOLENCE

Young people in many countries are experiencing high levels of depression. Statistics on depression reveals that in the United States, "[a]pproximately 20 percent of teens experience depression before they reach adulthood, and between 10 to 15 percent suffer from symptoms at any one time" (Borchard, 2016). Canadian Mental Health Association (2017) estimates that 10 to 20 per cent of Canadian youth experience some mental health illness or disorder. This organization notes that "the total number of 12-19 year olds in Canada at risk for developing depression is a staggering 3.2 million" (Canadian Mental Health Association, 2017). In Australia, the figures are also high, as "one in seven young Australians experience a mental health condition" (Beyond Blue, 2016). In Britain, among 16-18 year olds, "1 in 10 young people experience a mental health disorder", with [a]nxiety and depression . . . (being the) most common mental health difficulties and these have high co-morbidity" (AnxietyUK, 2015).

## IMMEDIATE ATTENTION IMPORTANT

While most instances of depression can be relieved or resolved through appropriate attention, many young people do not disclose their experiences, and often parents, teachers and other adults miss the signs of depression in their young people. Consequences of depression often lead to suicide or violence, which are unnecessary acts that could be avoided. Having greater knowledge of what constitutes depression, its causes, consequences and possible solutions could go a long way to relieving suffering.

## NOT ALWAYS DEPRESSION

The symptoms of depression are similar in some respects to those of normal teenage anxiety. Depression can sometimes be the result of physical causes such as thyroid disease. It is for this reason that young people who display symptoms of depression should not self-diagnose, but should speak to their parents and possibly a doctor (Hales, July 21, 2014). However, it is important to know as much as possible about depression in order to take appropriate action. Since depression affects brain function and development, the longer depression continues, the greater the damage, some of which could be irreparable (Hales, July 21, 2014).

Many young people who suffer from depression may feel that they are outcasts, and display aggressive behavior. At the same time, it should be noted that there is an increasing number of young people who appear to be fine, but who suffer their depression in silence.

## NOT JUST MOOD SWINGS

Many adults dismiss depression in youth as only mood swings, arguing that as time passes, the young person would get over whatever is ailing him or her. However, there are real causes for depression. Some of the factors that lead to depression include a difficult family life, persistent conflict within the family, a miserable childhood and behavioural problems. Some psychologists believe difficulties in school, problems with academic learning and behavior, attention deficit disorder (ADD), attention deficit and hyperactivity disorder (ADHD), and disruptive behavior are some of the conditions that could contribute to depression. According to Maag and Reid (2006), "[r]esearchers have found that students with learning disabilities (LD) obtain statistically higher scores on measures of depression than their peers without LD" (p. 3).

## DEPRESSION MORE COMMON AMONG GIRLS

Studies reveal that both boys and girls report depression and anxiety before puberty, but these conditions are more commonly seen among girls after puberty (Thapar, 2012). Depression is also shown to be associated with learning disorders. The rates of learning disorders among school-aged boys and girls were equivalent, but more boys and young men were referred to mental health clinics because of violent behavior. It is possible that males tend to externalize their problems and to manifest these through violent and aggressive behavior, whereas females tend to internalize these, and become depressed. As boys and girls become adolescents, the trend becomes more marked, with males being clearly identified as being more aggressive than females, and with females being more identified as suffering from depression.

## SOME SYMPTOMS OF DEPRESSION

Some of the feelings associated with depression are feelings of hopelessness, sadness, low self-esteem, sluggishness, substance base, wanting to spend more time alone, a decrease in desire for activities that were once enjoyable, physical ailments like headaches and problems with appetite and sleep, loss of interest in one's appearance, thoughts about death and suicide, and running away from home (Borchard, 2016). Besides these, other symptoms that could be used to suggest depression are poor performance at school, anger and rage, lack of enthusiasm, energy or motivation, over-reaction at criticism, feelings of being unable to satisfy ideals, guilt, indecision, lack of concentration and forgetfulness, restlessness and agitation, and problems with authority (Mental Health America, 2017).

## SOME FACTORS RELATED TO DEPRESSION

Several factors are implicated in depression. Some young people become involved in drug and alcohol use and other delinquent behavior because of depression, but these activities are also thought to trigger depression. In fact, many young people become involved in alcohol because of curiosity or because of peer pressure, and begin to demonstrate signs of depression. The easy availability of alcohol also makes alcohol the gateway to other drugs.

## DRUG ABUSE AND DEPRESSION

According to experts on drug abuse, the earlier a person starts using drugs, the more difficult the relationship with parents, the greater the depression, and the lower the self-esteem. This is increased further with more family conflict. Some risk factors for depression include the age of onset of addiction, as well as ineffective parenting and early childhood physical and/or sexual abuse. Some risk factors for drug abuse include learning difficulties, behavior problems, and influence by other young people who use drugs. These are also factors that could lead to depression.

## CYBERBULLYING AND DEPRESSION

While there are many other causes or factors that contribute to the onslaught of depression, one major one that should be considered is that of cyber bullying. With information drawn from 2015 National Survey on Drug Use and Health in the United States, Project Know (2016) reports that "[c]yberbullying ... affects over half of young people today." It is further pointed out that research into the effects of cyberbullying suggests that almost "14 percent of students facing cyberbullying attacks have a "severe or traumatic" reaction to the teasing or name calling that may continue for weeks or months without a parent or teacher being aware" (ProjectKnow, 2016). This observation shows the seriousness of cyberbullying and the effects it could have on young people, but also the fact that parents and other adults often do not see the signs that would indicate to them that their young people may need counselling, therapy or other treatment because of depression.

## RESILIENCY PAYS OFF

The fact that a young person finds himself or herself in a difficult situation does not mean that he or she has to succumb to what is taking place in the immediate environment. There are many young people who live in family settings where there are incidents of depression and violence, and who are able to develop healthy lifestyles. The explanation provided by Elisei, Sciarma, Verdolini and Anastasi (2013), is that some people have vulnerabilities that cause them to respond negatively and to develop psychiatric disorders, while there are other people who ae able to show resiliency and can remain intact and not succumb to psychiatric disorders like depression.

## ALWAYS THINK OF YOURSELF AS GOOD AND SPECIAL

If you are going through a difficult time, think of yourself as someone who is good and special. Don't let circumstances rob you of your self-worth. In the meantime, speak to someone who can help you deal with your depression. Seek professional help and you could start by seeing your family doctor, your school social worker or counsellor. Have faith in yourself and in the future. For those of us who believe in God, in the Almighty, or in a positive spiritual force, we have faith not only in ourselves, but in a greater power to help us through our difficult times and to give us strength to move ahead.

## HELPING A DEPRESSED FRIEND

According to Mental Health America (2017), three are ways of helping other young people who may be depressed. First, offer help and listen: while encouraging the friend to talk, one should refrain from lecturing the friend. Second, trust your instincts: when the situation seems serious, the recommendation is to break confidence and get help for the friend. Third, according to this organization, "Pay attention to talk about suicide. Ask direct questions and don't be afraid of frank discussions. Silence is deadly" (Mental Health American, 2017). The fourth point is to "seek professional help". Mental Health America (2017) maintains: "It is essential to seek expert advice from a mental health professional who has experience helping depressed teens. Also, alert key adults in the teen's life – family, friends, and teachers." In other words, one must give help to a friend when one sees a potential for crisis, even when one may have agreed not tell another person about the self-injury that another teen or young person may be planning. Above all, be a friend to someone who needs a friend.

## BE A FRIEND TO SOMEONE IN NEED

As a young person, you can be a friend to someone who is going through a difficult time. You can be kind to someone, and this can make the difference at a crucial point in that person's life. When a boy at his school had dropped a whole pile of books as he was cleaning out his locker, Steve bent down and helped the boy pick up his books. He had not remembered this until several years later, when this boy, now a young man, met Steve on the street, and greeted him as an old friend. For a while, Steve was stunned, but the young man told Steve that the day that he had bent down and help him pick up his books, he felt that he had a friend in the world. This was significant to that young man, for at the time that this happened, he was contemplating suicide, and was cleaning out his locker so that his mother would not have to do it after his death. Steve's kindness had actually changed the young boy's mind, because he began thinking that he had a friend.

# CHAPTER 14: *REFERENCES AND FURTHER READING*

Albert, P. R. (2015). Why is depression more prevalent in women? *Journal of Psychiatry & Neuroscience, 40*(4), 219-221.

AnxietyUK (2015). Young people and anxiety. Retrieved from *https://www.anxietyuk.org.uk/our-services/anxiety-information/young-people-and-anxiety/*

Beyond Blue (2016). Stats and Facts (on Depression and Anxiety in Australia). Retrieved from *https://www.youthbeyondblue.com/footer/stats-and-facts*

Borchard, T. J. (2016). So why are so many teens depressed? Psych Central. World of Psychology. Retrieved from https://psychcentral.com/blog/archives/2010/03/04/why-are-so-many-teens-depressed/

Canadian Mental Health Association (2017). Fast facts about mental illness. Retrieved from *http://www.cmha.ca/media/fast-facts-about-mental-illness/*

Elisei, S., Sciarma, T. Verdolini, N. & Anastasi, S. (2013). Resilience and depressive disorders. *Psychiatria Danubina, 25* Suppl 2:S263-267.

Hales, E. (July 21, 2014).  Understanding and responding to the increase in teen depression. *Desert News.* Retrieved from http://www.deseretnews.com/article/865607079/Understanding-and-responding-to-the-increase-of-adolescent-depression.html

Maag, J. W. & Reid, R. (2006). Depression among students with learning disabilities: Assessing the risk. *Journal of Learning Disabilities, 39*(1), 3-10

Mental Health America (2017). Depression in Teens. Retrieved from *http://www.mentalhealthamerica.net/conditions/depression-teens*

ProjectKnow (2016). Teens and Depression: Exploring major depressive  episodes among youth. Retrieved from *http://www.projectknow.com/discover/depression-among-youth/*

Thapar, A., Cikkishaw, S., Pine, D. S. & Thapar, A. K. (2012). Depression in adolescence. *Lancet, 379*(9820), 1056-1067.

# CHAPTER 15

# HEALING AN OOZING SORE – YOUTH CRIME

Most youths are responsible young people, who are looking forward to a bright future. They are undertaking the appropriate education and training to prepare them for the roles they see themselves performing as adults. Many young people are eager to take on adult roles, and they approach this with a sense of responsibility and excitement.

However, there are some young people who are in dire straits and who do not see the world with such optimism and hope. It is some of these young people that may simply have given up and some may even have become engaged in youth crime. One of the observations is that although both young males and females engage in such activity, the majority of youth crime is carried out by males (Karriker-Jaffe, Foshee, Ennett, & Suchindran, 2008).

## ADDRESSING YOUTH VIOLENCE

We often excuse youth as the actions of the young and the immature, and sometimes as mental illness that has not been addressed. In many cases, because of the ages of the young people, we withhold their names as a means of protecting them during this "formative" period. In effect, what we are doing in some instances is excusing them and not holding youths accountable for the adult crimes that they may have committed. Unless we look at the 'sore', diagnose the causes honestly, and apply the appropriate dressing to bring about healing, the 'sore' of youth crime will continue to fester.

## OF COURSE, SOME YOUTHS NEED PROTECTION

There are some young people who engage in criminal behavior through ignorance or otherwise, who are repentant of their actions, who change their ways and who could benefit from more lenient treatment under the legal system. But this should be the exception rather than the rule.

## WHAT WE ALREADY KNOW

What do we know from many of these studies? Young people who become involved in crime are not happy. Most are not excelling in school, and many are failing or have already dropped out of school. Most have no marketable skills, and many feel alienated in society. Many youths who engage in criminal activity feel excluded by their peers for any number of reasons, including poverty, race/ethnicity, lack of popularity, poor social skills, lack of attention, or some difference. Many minority youth who are involved in criminal activity may also feel excluded because of discrimination and racism, while many minority and non-minority youths who become involved in criminal activity may feel alienated, excluded, and hopeless, with few opportunities available to them.

## SOME MAJOR CAUSES

We learn that poverty is a major issue, with unemployment highest among youth in the 15 – 24 age range (Statistics Canada), and the very age when many young people are trying to become independent. Many who become involved with criminal activity use drug-dealing as a means of making a living. Drug abuse also involves criminal behavior. According to Chung and Steinberg (2006), peer relations, neighbourhood factors, and parenting factors are some of the other factors that are associated with youth criminal behaviour.

## LACK OF NURTURING AND SELF-RESPECT

Youths may become involved in criminal activity for lack of nurturing and/or to gain attention. Youth crime is also associated with a lack of respect for others and for life, and with the misplaced search for self-respect in violence, as evident when a youth kills another to prove that he is a man.

## WE KNOW ALL THIS

We know all this. We know the symptoms and we have the diagnoses: low levels of education, lack of marketable skills, a serious lack of employment opportunities, poverty, racism, alienation, lack of respect for others and for life, and the resulting effects of hopelessness and desperation. Any number of these symptoms could lead to youth crime.

## POSSIBLE SOLUTIONS

To heal the oozing sore of youth crime, we have to address these problems as a society, both adults and young people. Parents who know of their children's criminal activity must take steps to help their children. Young people must also take responsibility for their actions, knowing that there are consequences that can have life-changing effects. As a society, we have to take genuine and serious steps to deal with youth crime and not become preoccupied with appearing to be doing something about it.

## MORE ACTION NEEDED

Action involves helping to equip young people with education and marketable skills, helping them to become employed and self-sufficient, reversing the effects of racism and discrimination where these are problems, providing nurturing environments, building a strong self-image, and instilling a healthy respect for others, for self, and for life.

## A YOUNG PERSON'S RESPONSIBILITY

If you are a young person who finds yourself caught up in criminal activity, STOP and THINK! Do you have a low level of education, can't find a job because you have no skills, and as a result you feel hopeless? Are these some of the conditions that have led you to your present situation? STOP and THINK again. Even if things look hopeless, they are not. YOU COULD MAKE A RIGHT-ABOUT TURN. You are better than you think you are. The fact that you are here, alive, is a privilege. You are unique and special. You are the only You there is. BE THANKFUL. You have the privilege of making a contribution to your society, in a way that only you could do.  Yes, maybe things are not going well for you now.  Maybe you didn't receive a good education and were not born into comfortable means.

## THERE ARE OPPORTUNITIES

Take comfort.  You are young, and you can make changes now. One man who wanted to learn to read so badly, and never had the opportunity to do so, took the chance to learn to read when he was in his 90s.  If someone could learn at that age, just think of what you can do now! Nothing is too difficult if you put your mind to it.  Remember, there are many people willing to help you get back on tract! Start with your family members or friends!

## IT'S NOT TOO LATE – THERE IS HOPE

You may say: "I am already involved in crime.  There is no way I can clean up my act."  NOT TRUE.  Judge Greg Mathis, who is presently a judge in the United States, got involved in criminal activity as a youth.  His mother made sure that when he committed a crime he paid the price. She called police and he went to jail.  However, one day, when his mother told him she was going to die, he smartened up.  He made a RIGHT-ABOUT TURN, stopped getting involved in criminal activity, and started paying attention to his education.  Today, he is a judge.  He proved that it is possible to clean up one's act and live a respectable life.  YOU CAN DO IT, TOO. Just imagine how very impressive your life could be, if you MAKE A RIGHT-ABOUT TURN and prove to the world and to yourself that you are really someone special.  Think of the influence you could have on many younger people by showing them how to do something special with their lives!

## DON'T BLOW YOUR CHANCES

When you become involved in criminal activity, you are actually blowing your chances for making your positive contribution, and for being the 'BEST YOU' THERE IS. Don't sell yourself short. You are worth being THE BEST YOU CAN BE.

## BE THE BEST YOU CAN BE

As a young person involved in criminal activity, you must take action on your behalf, realizing that you have a purpose for being here. Not doing anything positive with your life amounts to not carrying out the worthy purpose for which you were created. You have to take stock of where you are and where you want to get to in life. It won't happen if you do nothing.

## WHERE TO START

WHERE TO START? If you are a young person involved in criminal activity, decide that YOU WILL CHANGE YOUR LIFE. Then think of improving your education. Maybe you aren't sure what to do or where to start. Ask someone. Speak to a responsible and positive adult, a minister, a rabbi, a religious leader, a teacher, a social worker, a librarian, a school counsellor, a probation officer, a grandparent, or a parent. There are many other people who would be all too willing to help you, or to find the right help for you. If you don't get the right help from one person, ask someone else, because there is help available.

# CHAPTER 15 - REFERENCES AND FURTHER READING

Brown, S. (2005). Understanding youth and crime: Listening to youth. Open University Press.

Chung, H. L. & Steinberg, L. (2006). Relations between neighborhood factors, parenting behaviors, peer deviance, and delinquency among serious juvenile offenders. *Developmental Psychology, 42*(2), 319-331.

Cody, C. (2013). A new response to youth crime. *British Journal of Community Justice,* 10(3).

Gifford-Smith, M., Dodge, K. A., Dishion, T. J., & McCord, J. (2005). Peer influence in children and adolescents: Crossing the bridge from developmental to intervention science. *Journal of Abnormal Child Psychology, 33*(3), 255-265.

Karriker-Jaffe, K, J., Foshee, V. A., Ennett, S. T. & Suchindran, C. (2008). The development of aggression during adolescence: Sex differences in trajectories of physical and social aggression among youth in rural areas. *Journal of Abnormal Child Psychology, 36*(8), 1227-1228.

Mathis, Judge Greg (2002). *The Inner City Miracle.* New York: Ballantine.

Moore, M. D. & Sween, M. (2015). Rural youth crime: A reexamination of social disorganization theory's applicability to rural areas. *Journal of Juvenile Justice, 4*(1).

Rud, I., Van Klaveren, C., Groot, W., & van den Brink, H. M. (2013). Education and youth crime: a review of the empirical literature. *The Working Paper Series, Tier WP 13/06.* Mastricht University, Amsterdam, 1-32.

Scott, E. S. & Steinberg, L. (2008). Adolescent development and the regulation of youth crime. *The Future of Children, 18*(2).

Smyth, G. (2010). "What have we done right?" Targets and youth crime prevention. British *Journal of Community Justice, 8*(1)

CHAPTER 16

# TREATING THE SYMPTOMS, NOT THE DISEASE – YOUTH CRIME

## HOW TO DEAL WITH YOUTH CRIME

Many would agree that there is much talk about youth crime, but not enough talk about why it is happening and what to do about it. Instead of finding long-term and concrete solutions to the problem, we use what we perceive as short-term solutions. What we are actually doing is taking a similar approach to dealing with youth crime as we use dealing with several illnesses. We address the symptoms.

Our approach to medicine is often criticized as treating the symptoms and not the disease. We have been conditioned to take a tablet when we have a headache. If one tablet doesn't work, we could always find another that will. We are not particularly interested in finding out why we had the headache in the first place, but primarily in soothing the pain. And the list goes on.

## TREATING THE SYMPTOMS OF YOUTH CRIME

We seem to be taking this approach with many other conditions, including youth violence, particularly male youth violence. We continue to engage in discussions on how to deal with the problem, without fully investigating why this is happening. We have tried, and are still trying, various solutions, but these solutions focus on the symptoms of the disease, without trying to identify and treat the disease itself. We see suspensions and incarceration used to deal with youth crime, but with little or no effect.

## ZERO TOLERANCE

We have introduced zero tolerance to violence in our schools, and to achieve this, we suspend or expel our violent students. We get rid of violence in schools, or at least we get rid of some of it. This is just like taking a tablet for a recurring headache, but not finding out why the headache occurred, and realizing that the head persists.

## INCARCERATION

Another approach to dealing with male youth violence is to incarcerate those that are violent and those that are caught. We hold them in institutions for a couple of months, even when they commit violent crimes, because they are often "young offenders". Even when we could classify them as adult offenders and try them in adult courts, we imprison them – primarily holding them for a period of time. This is again similar to taking another type of tablet. Then we release these violent individuals into the society again, and when the effects of the tablet have worn off, they re-offend. In some instances, some individuals who may not have committed a crime are held unjustly for an indefinite period of time, only to be released several years later, bitter. The result is that very often incarceration of young people does not work, particularly if they were not guilty in the first place, but even if they were offenders, they may often be released without any improvement in their condition. The likelihood of reoffending is high.

## VIOLENCE AND CRIMINAL ACTIVITY CONTINUE

This is how I see the situation. There is nothing wrong with trying to soothe the pain of a severe toothache by taking a tablet. It could bring relief relatively quickly, but be sure, the pain is going to return. Similarly, using one or some of these measures to curb male youth violence may bring some relief to the problem, but this is all that it would bring – relief - and this is generally a temporary condition. Of course, there are some young people that may have made a mistake and that may be diverted from the criminal justice system by some leniency.

## LEAVING THE ROOT PROBLEMS INTACT

However, it is my opinion that we are dealing with the symptoms and leaving the root causes of the disease of male youth violence untouched. Suspending or expelling a student or having more surveillance would not deal with why we have so much male youth violence to begin with. These measures only push the problem deeper underground to manifest itself, to our dismay, in even more horrendous ways.

## HIGH TIME FOR CHANGE

Let us face it. For too long, we have been using 'tablets' to solve the problem of male youth violence, and have not been looking for, or dealing with, the root causes of the problem. Consequently, we have not been able to bring about a genuine healing of the disease. We need to deal more effectively with youth crime, not by throwing young people into jail and forgetting them until it is time to release them into society again, but by rehabilitating, training and retraining for jobs in the society, and by preventing their incarceration in the first place with programs aimed at giving young people hope and the opportunity to make a good living in society.

When we deprive them of an opportunity of building a good and profitable career by ensuring their education, we create the motivation for criminal activity. After all, all human beings seek the means of bettering themselves and when they cannot find it the legal way, they will choose illegal ways of doing this. It is this activity that becomes classified as criminality.

# CHAPTER 16 - REFERENCES AND FURTHER READING

Baron, S. W. (2004). General Strain, street youth and crime: A test of Agnew's revised theory. *Criminology*, 42(2), 457-483.

Case, C., Creany, S., Deakin, J. & Haines, K. (2015). Youth justice: Past, present and future. *British Journal of Community Justice, 13*(2), 99 - 110

Cook, P. J. & Jens, L. (2004). Does gun prevalence affect teen gun carrying after all? *Criminology*, 42(1), 27-54.

Dominey, J. (2011). Breaking the cycle: The government response. *British Journal of Community Justice, 9*(1-2), 119-122.

Fox, K. A. (2013). New developments and implications for understanding the victimization of gang members. *Violence and Victims, 28*(6), 1015-1040

# CHAPTER 17

# LOOKING AT THE GUN ISSUE

How many young men must die in gang warfare? How many innocent bystanders must be hurt or killed by the callous and cowardly acts of unscrupulous individuals? How many mothers and fathers must weep at the deaths of their children, gang-related casualties related to the drug trade, or innocent victims of mass shootings? In light of these situations, guns are surely not an option. Although we point to the Second Amendment provision in the United States as guaranteeing our right to own guns, the use of guns in criminality is not sanctioned by the Constitution.

## PURPOSE OF GUNS

Think about it! What purpose does a gun serve? To kill, or at best, to maim. Police officers, in their role to "protect and serve", are equipped with better guns simply to keep up with the level of sophistication of the weapons criminals carry around today. Criminals, and young misguided 'wanna-be's', see guns as an equalizer for their perceived inadequacies. Law-abiding citizens see the carrying of guns as their constitutional right and maintain that guns are for sport, even for killing animals which they eat, and perchance for protection. But the argument that is often made is that law-abiding citizens may need their guns for protection . . . from other human beings . . . criminals.

## THINK ABOUT IT!

But think about it again! People killing other people for fame, for revenge, or for material possessions, is truly barbaric. Killing other people so that they would not steal property also seems barbaric. Stealing other people's property is also unacceptable behavior. However, when pitting human life against material possessions, we do not put much store on human life.

## WE ARE SUPPOSED TO BE AN ADVANCED CIVILIZATION

In an age when humans have the thinking capacity to create computers, to map the human genome, to send rockets into space, and to actually maintain residence on a planet other than earth, some humans are still scurrying around like cavemen with their clubs. Only, this time, these individuals are scurrying around with guns.

## CAVEMEN – SUPERIOR ABILITY

Significantly, when cavemen wielded clubs, they exhibited superior ability to those individuals today who brandish guns. The reason? Cavemen used clubs primarily for securing food, a critical act of survival. In our society, many of our young men (and some women) who use guns are working against the law of nature that made cavemen carry clubs. These young people who carry guns are choosing death or extinction rather than survival, as all living species are supposed to do.

## GUNS AND MENTAL ILLNESS

Some may argue that many of the cases of gun violence involve the use of young people who are mentally ill. Many cases of mass shootings in schools, malls, and other public places have often been traced to individuals who may have felt wronged in some way, who were bullied, who wanted revenge, or who were said to be mentally imbalanced. Some may also have been influenced by gun violence portrayed in videos.

## GUNS OBTAINED LEGALLY

Many of these individuals obtained their guns legally and were exercising their constitutional right to own a gun. Or they may have obtained their guns from family members who were legally allowed to have guns. Therefore, generally when these instances happen, we look to the factors that may have caused the young person to commit such an act.

## ILLEGAL GUNS

Those who stress the importance of protecting their gun rights point to the fact that many crimes, usually those associated with property crimes and the drug trade, are carried out with illegal guns. These are guns that may have been smuggled into the country. The argument that is being made is that it is not legal guns that should be the target of legislation, but the illegal guns coming into the country.

## REALLY TWO PROBLEMS

The fascination of our society with guns may be at the heart of the problem. Many mass shootings involve the use of guns legally acquired and many property crimes and drug trading involves the use of illegal guns.

## DEALING WITH MASS SHOOTINGS

In the case of the use of legal guns used in mass shootings, we should be very concerned with how available guns are to people who may be depressed, angry, and who may be mentally ill.  Means should be found for gun owners to have greater control over their guns.  There is also a responsibility to keep guns away from family members who we know are not mentally stable. We need to close loopholes that would allow unstable individuals to obtain guns legally. People with criminal past should be prevented from legally owning guns.  These are all measures that need to be put in place. Even if it means restricting gun rights, this could be seen as a sensible measure.

## DEALING WITH MENTAL ILLNESS

More measures should be put in place for dealing with mental illness. Even when parents know that there is something mentally wrong with their children, getting help seems to be a major hurdle that many cannot overcome. Consequently, there are many individuals living with family members that are mentally ill and without getting the right help for them.  In some instances, individuals with mental illness are not diagnosed, because there are not an adequate number of accessible clinics that would allow for such diagnosis.  As a society, we have to think of the measures needed to deal with this. More funding should be provided by public and private institutions to deal with this illness.

## DEALING WITH ILLEGAL GUNS

The issue of illegal guns is closely tied up with the issue of illegal drugs and the vast drug trading that is taking place. Many of the drugs that come into the country illegally are brought in by gangs and other illegal operators, but many officials in high places are thought to be turning a blind eye to the drugs entering the country, because of the payments and bribes. Some of those in positions of authority may be themselves involved in the importation of drugs because of the financial rewards. Shame on them. Very stringent measures should be taken to cut out the illegal drug trade and when individuals who organize the trade are caught, they should be treated so harshly that others are discouraged. Reduction in the drug trade would very likely lead to a reduction in the trade in illegal drugs.

## REDUCING THE ILLEGAL DRUG TRADE

This practice of simply letting out the top drug kingpins after they are caught will only continue this trade. Locking up the scores of small drug dealers cannot solve the problem, because other small drug dealers could be easily found. When these small drug dealers are caught, they should be thought of as the small branches that could lead to the main trunk of the drug trade. The main dealers could lead to the sources from which the drugs are coming, and these sources should be targeted for eradication.

## LEGALIZATION OF SOME DRUGS

Some jurisdictions have introduced legalization of marijuana as a means of targeting the drug trade, believing that if some drugs are legalized, then there would be no need for an illegal trade, and would cut down on the illegal gun trade and use associated with illegal drugs. This is a rather controversial topic that still needs to be discussed.

## DON'T FORGET POSSIBLE INFLUENCE OF VIDEO GAMES

Some mass shootings have been likened to scenes in video games, with some perpetrators of mass shootings, as occurred in Columbine, mentioning the influence of video games on their actions. However, while the research about the possible influence of violent video games on violent behavior is not conclusive, some people, because of their susceptibility, may be influenced. Young people who play these games are the best evaluators of how video games affect them, and should make decisions about their use of these media.

## IN THE MEANTIME

Every young person needs to give this subject of guns a serious consideration. When the subject of guns are raised, as a society we take a very emotional approach, believing that our gun rights would be restricted, and that we would no longer have guns. Many of us cannot have a clear discussion about the pros and cons about guns, and are unable to look clearly at the different aspects of the issue reasonably.

While mostly older people are the ones that are adamant about our constitutional right to own guns, it is the younger generations that are really the ones that are mostly involved in the gun issue. The younger generations are the ones mostly involved in mass shootings, as perpetrators and as victims. It is the younger generations that are the ones that are diagnosed as having mental illness and are using guns to wreak havoc on others. It is the younger generations that are mostly involved in the use of illegal guns and the illegal drug trade. It is mostly the younger generations that consume the majority of violent video games.

## FINDING SOLUTIONS RELATED TO GUNS

Young people, whoever you are, open your eyes and choose survival, according to the law of nature. Think of the gun issue and the many arguments that are raised about owning guns, using guns, preventing dangerous possession of guns, and using illegal drugs and the associated use of illegal guns. These are all topics that young people need to think about and not only allow older people to tell you what to do.

## THIS IS YOUR WORLD, NOW AND IN THE FUTURE

You must think for yourselves and find solutions that would improve the society and prevent the countless lives that are lost daily from gun use. After all, this is your world and within a couple decades, you will be the older people. Start now to prepare the kind of world you want to live in now and in the future.

# CHAPTER 17 - REFERENCES AND FURTHER READING

Aliprantis, D. & Chen, A. (2016). The consequences of exposure to violence during early childhood. Economic Commentary, 2016(3), 1-6.

America's gun problem is so much bigger than mass shootings (June 21, 2016). Guardian. Retrieved from *https://www.theguardian.com/us-news/2016/jun/21/gun-control-debate-mass-shootings-gun-violence*

Kozuskanich, N. (2009). Originalism in a digital age: An inquiry into the right to bear arms. *Journal of the Early Republic, 29*(4), 585-606.

Melzer, S. (2009). *Gun Crusaders: The NRA's culture war.* New York: New York University Press.

# CHAPTER 18

# WHEN ENOUGH SHOULD BE ENOUGH: WHEN MEN BEAT WOMEN

Some young women live in conditions of physical and emotional abuse, and have many excuses for enduring this abuse. Some women with children take the position that they are doing it for their children's sake. Others sustain this lifestyle because they claim they love their partners too much and can't do without them. Others remain in abusive situations because they believe their abusing partners can't do without them. They also believe that they can help these abusing partners become reformed. Some young women stay in abusive situations because of material considerations, depending on their partners to provide money for necessities. Many young girls get entangled with abusive boyfriends because they may be afraid of not having a boyfriend, or of not being loved. Some women stay because, as they point out, they have no way to make a living, and no place to live.

## NOT A STABLE ENVIRONMENT

The young women who remain in abusive situations because of their children believe that they are providing a stable family life for their children, a family consisting of both parents. Although a two-parent family is promoted as ideal, it is not ideal under many conditions. As some experts say, abuse is one of those conditions. It is better to be in a single-parent family where there is love and caring, and where children are taught about respect for each other, than to be in a two-parent family where there is fighting, abuse and disrespect.

## CHILD ABUSE

Some children are also abused in these relationships. Researchers claim that children from abusive homes are more likely to grow up to be abusive themselves. As one source points out, children who grew up in abusive situations as in domestic violence become adolescents and adults who are also likely to be abusive and the chances are they would even abuse their children (Jouriles, McDonald, Slep, Heyman & Garrido, 2008).

## CHILDREN LEARN ABUSE AND BULLYING

It does not matter whether the abuse is physical or emotional, children learn unconsciously how to behave, how to interrelate with others, and how to cope with situations from what they see exhibited around them. Staying in an abusive relationship for the sake of the children, and not seeking help for this dysfunctional relationship for the sake of love, is destructive to all concerned. In fact, many experts claim that children learn bullying from living in these situations (Jouriles et al., 2008).

Many young women do not have children to use as an excuse for being in an abusive relationship. Many of these younger women make their sacrifice 'for love'. They claim that their love for their boyfriend is unconditional, and so justify their remaining in the abusive relationship, hoping to help these boyfriends. They rationalize that they cannot bear to take away their 'love' from these boyfriends who cannot help themselves.

## UNCONDITIONAL LOVE NOT ENOUGH

Some women believe that despite the abuse, their partners need them and would not make it without them being around. These women seem to have a need to save the men that they believe are helpless. It is not enough for a young woman to be so desperate to feel needed and loved that she will accept abuse. Someone who is abusing a young woman is actually saying by his actions that he doesn't need her. It is time for a young woman who is made to feel as if she is worth nothing to move on.

## 'SAVING-THE-HELPLESS' MENTALITY

Some young women stay in abusive situations because of material things. They continue taking abuse because they are dependent. They believe that they cannot make it on their own. While some admit financial dependence, others contend that it is not material need that keeps them in abusive relationships. Young women need to see themselves as capable of taking care of themselves.

## STAY FOR MATERIALISTIC CONSIDERATION

Many women deny that they use excuses to stay in these relationships. Some women believe they cannot leave an abusive situation because they have nowhere to go. However, shelters are available to help women who are being abused, and who need safe places to get away from that abuse. These shelters provide not only a safe place, but also different types of counselling as well as life-skills training for adjustment to a new lifestyle.

## NOWHERE TO GO

However, according to researchers, despite the availability of shelters, many women are abused over and over, sometimes to the point of sustaining serious physical injury, and sometimes even risking death, before they decide to leave for good. Others never leave, and pay the price with their lives.

## ABUSE IS LEARNED

Women who stay in abusive relationships are actually making a big sacrifice, one that deprives them of self-esteem, of dignity and of self-respect. Those with children are exposing their children to developing a similar pattern of behavior, as children imitate their parents' behaviour. Researchers point out that abuse is learned. In many instances where young women accept abuse and where young men mete out this abuse, both sides exhibit behaviours that were learned in childhood (Jouriles et al., 2008). They have come to accept the abuse as normal behaviour, since this is what they may have seen around them most of their lives.

## NOTHING NORMAL ABOUT ABUSE

However, this behavior is not normal, and this is why young men and young women who are caught up in a web of violence, need to break free.

## "WHY AM I HERE?"

Regardless of the excuse for staying in a physically or emotionally abusive relationship, younger and older women should wake up and realize that they are individuals who are worthy of love and respect. When respect is lacking, love is seldom present. Abuse, physical or emotional, is a demonstration of a lack of love. If you are in an abusive relationship, ask yourself, "Why am I here?" Experts claim that if you look back into your past, you may see the conditions that may have made you choose to stay in this relationship (Raeder, 2014).

## PUTTING YOURSELF IN THE PICTURE

Did you have abuse in your own family as a child? Did you accept abuse in earlier relationships and see this as 'normal' behavior? If you answer "Yes" to any of these questions, and if you have children, think about the effect your relationship may be having on them. Even if your children are very young, or do not see the abuse, they are still aware of it happening.

## TAKE ACTION NOW

If you are a young girl whose boyfriend is abusing her, don't make excuses for his behavior. Abuse does not demonstrate love, but in fact demonstrates lack of respect and caring. Get out of the abusive situation before you are more seriously hurt, emotionally or physically. Leave the abusive relationship, because you are a special and worthwhile person, and need to be treated in a special way.

## THEN THERE IS THE ISSUE OF SEXUAL ASSAULT – DATE RAPE

Rape is never right or acceptable. Today, there are many reports about date rape and assault of young women, and the question that is being asked is whether there is an increase in these incidents or whether women (and some men) are having the strength to speak up about their experiences. Regardless of the reason for this increase in reporting, many young people are realizing and acknowledging that sexual assault is a gross violation of a person's rights.

## NEED TO OFFER A HELPING HAND

Usually, the perpetrators are young men, who pride themselves on their physical prowess. Unfortunately, some of these young men are good and aspiring athletes. In reality, they are selfish and unethical individuals who prey on young women. Even if a young woman is impaired by alcohol or drugs, the responsible and ethical thing for a young man to do is to lend a helping hand rather than seeing it as an opportunity for raping or violating that young woman's rights.

## ENOUGH IN THE NEWS

The consequences for such actions are well documented, with reports of young men who were caught in the act or who were linked to the act being sent to jail. Some may say, "What a terrible way for a young man to end his career." However, at the same time, what they should be saying instead is, "What a terrible way for a young woman's life to be marred by such an unthinking act!"

## ENOUGH IS ENOUGH

If you are a young man who is abusing his girlfriend, you need to make changes immediately. No one has the right to abuse another. You may need to speak to a counsellor with respect to your abusive behaviour, and possibly seek anger management or other therapy that may be recommended!

If you have ever taken advantage of a girl who is impaired through alcohol or drugs, or if you forced yourself on a girl in the past, acknowledge that what you did was rape. It was not a youthful indiscretion, but rather a crime. If nothing came of it, even though it may have been reported to the university or college, this is not a victory for you, but a gross failure or negligence. The fact remains, you have committed a crime. You have to stop doing this. Be respectful to the girls that you date. They are not to be part of your conquests. Remember, without mutual consent, there should be no sexual involvement. Anything short of this is rape, a crime that could get you jail time.

Jackson Katz, who is described as "a leading anti-sexist male activist," has done ground-breaking work with men and boys on gender-violence prevention. He has put forward some great ideas on how men and boys can take a very active role in preventing violence against all women as well as men who may not be heterosexual. As Katz (2013) observes, they should "[a]pproach gender violence as a men's issue involving men of all ages and socioeconomic, racial, and ethnic backgrounds. View men not only as perpetrators or possible offenders, but as empowered bystanders who can confront abusive peers" (p. 523, in Hobbs & Rice, 2013).

For young women, it is important to know your rights. It is also important to be in control of your person, and be very specific about your intentions with your date. Don't be afraid to say "No". If he becomes angry or refuse to date you in the future, because you refuse to have sex with him. Then, maybe, he was only with you for sex.

Young men! Young women! Think! And think before you act.

## CHAPTER 18 - REFERENCES AND FURTHER READING

Belshaw, S. H., Siddique, J.A., Tanner, J. & Osho, G. S. (2012). The relationship between dating violence and suicidal behaviors in a national sample of adolescents. *Violence and Victims, 27*(4), 580-591.

Boxall, H., Roseveau, L. & Payne, J. (2015). Domestic violence typologies: What value to practice. *Trends and Issues in Crime and Criminal Justice, 494.* *http://www.aic.gov.au/publications/current%20se ries/tandi/481-500/tandi494.html*

Dodich, C. & Siedlaz, M. (2014). Date rape drugs. *International Journal of Child and Adolescent Health, 7*(4), 355-368.

Jouriles, E. N., Mcdonald, R., Slep, A. M., Heyman, R. E., & Gardo, e. (2008). Child abuse in the context of domestic violence: Prevalence, explanations and practice implications. *Violence and Victims, 23*(2), 221-235.

Katz, J. (2013). Ten things men can do to prevent gender violence. In Hobbs, M. & Rice, C. (2013). Gender and women's studies in Canada: Critical terrain. Toronto: Women's Press.

Pryor, D. W. & Hughes, M. R. (2013). Fear of rape among college women: A social psychological analysis. *Violence and Victims, 28*(3), 443-465.

Raeder, M. S. (2014). Preserving families ties for domestic violence survivors and their children by invoking a human rights approach to avoid the criminalization of mothers based on the acts and accusations of their batterers. *The Journal of Gender, Race and Justice, 17*(1), 105.

Rao, T., Nagpel, M. & Andrade, C. (2013). Sexual coercion: Time to rise to the challenge. *Indian Journal of Psychiatry, 55*(3), 211-213.

Raphael, A. (2013). Rape is rape: How denial, distortion, and victim Blaming are fueling a hidden acquaintance rape crisis. Chicago, Illinois: Lawrence Hill Books.

Senn, C. Y. (2013). Education on resistance to acquaintance sexual assault: Preliminary promise of a new program for young women in high school and university. *Canadian Journal of Behavioural Science, 45*(1), 24-33.

Whitbeck, L. B., Hoyt, D. R., Johnson, K. D. & Chen, X. (2007). Victimization and posttraumatic stress disorder among runaway and homeless adolescents. *Violence and Victims, 22*(6), 721-734.

# CHAPTER 19

# NOT PLAYING FAIR - WHEN WOMEN BEAT MEN

Family violence is a common practice that was once thought of as a private matter, and so was guarded as a secret. In more recent times, it has become a public issue, as more and more women are willing to speak out about the abuse that they experience. Some men feel they have the right to 'control' their wives and girlfriends by whatever means possible. This includes not only beating or other forms of physical abuse, but also emotional abuse, such as belittling and humiliating. Both men and women abuse their children, physically and emotionally, again with the rationale that they have the right to 'control' them.

## WHEN WOMEN BEAT MEN

However, a condition that has existed for just as long, and that has received little attention, is that of the physical and emotional abuse of men by women. Just as some young men abuse their girlfriends, in the same way, some young women abuse their boyfriends, mistakenly believing that this is part of what being in love is all about. They see the making up after the abuse as something desirable.

## NOTHING TO SNICKER ABOUT

However, according to Hill (2004), there are many men who are being abused by their partners, physically as well as emotionally, and many of them are choosing to keep this a secret. The question that must be asked is why women and children are more willing to speak up, and men are not. The answer can be found in the stereotypical images that our society still holds about men and women. Men are seen as the ones that ought to be in control.

## ERROR IN JUDGEMENT

Sometime ago, a judge was 'reprimanded' for comments he made when presiding over a case of spousal abuse brought by a man against his wife. In a nutshell, the judge trivialized the charge, noting that the man 'should be a man' and not be pushed around by his wife. The wife more or less got off, because it was not seen as a major issue. The ridicule that a man who is beaten by his wife may receive for revealing this occurrence is sometimes seen as enough for him to decide to keep the abuse quiet, rather than retaliate by abusing his wife. This situation that some men face today parallel that of some women who, in the past, were afraid of speaking up in court, or in public, about the violence they experienced.

## WHAT THE LAW SAYS

The present-day law in many countries speaks of 'spousal abuse', which covers both men and women. Any person, male or female, could bring a charge of assault. Yet, many men are suffering in silence, for fear of being thought of 'as not being a man' and as being made a laughing stock by others.

## SOME THINK THIS IS CUTE

At the same time, many women 'hit' and seem to think that it is acceptable for them to do so. Many girls believe that it is 'cute' to hit their boyfriends.  It is not. This situation seems unfair.  When a man hits a woman, it's abuse. When a woman hits a man, a large part of society believes that it is nothing serious.  It is.

## A FAULTY EXPLANATION

The explanation that is sometimes given is that a man hits so much harder than a woman can. This may or may not be the case, but it is not the issue. Abuse is abuse. Besides, many women are not the stereotypically weak and delicate females, and can sometimes be as strong as or even stronger than their partners.  Some could deal a severe blow.

## A TASTE OF THEIR OWN MEDICINE?  MORE FAULTY THINKING

Another explanation often given is that women have been abused for decades, and some are still being abused today. "So what if some men are getting a taste of their own medicine," some may argue. This argument is not acceptable, either.   Spousal abuse is never justified, regardless of who has the role of the abuser.

## DOUBLE STANDARD NO LONGER ACCEPTABLE

Both men and women should be held accountable when they hit or assault another person. There should not be one rule for men and one for women. Double standards are no longer acceptable. In the 21st century, we should be thinking in a more sophisticated manner. We are thinking beings, capable of reasoning and making decisions. Why should we, either male or female, resort to physical violence as a means of solving problems? Violence does not work: the problems still remain.

## STEREOTYPES PERSIST

What do these different perceptions of male and female abuse really say? It says that we are still thinking in a stereotypical manner, that we still see women as inferior to men. It also says that we still see the action or behaviour of women as inconsequential or as not counting for much. Although some men are on the receiving end, this thinking still relegates women to a stereotypically inferior position.

## NEED TO PLAY FAIR

We need to play fair, to see men and women as equal partners, with the same potential, the same abilities and the same responsibilities. If we play fair, in time men and women would treat each other equally and with respect, and we would be all better off because of it. We should therefore appeal to both men and women to stop abusing each other and their children. However, from the statistics, more women fall victim to abuse from boyfriends and husbands.

## CONDEMN ABUSE

Young men and young women, you should see abuse as something undesirable. You would then have the opportunity to grow up respecting each other and believing that you have the same potential. Young women and young men, as you enter into your intimate relationships, remember that you have the power to form good and healthy relationships, regardless of whether or not you were brought up in abusive homes. Do not use an early, abusive home life as an excuse for remaining in an abusive and disrespectful relationship. Respect and love go hand in hand, and when respect is missing, often love is also missing.

If you have been a survivor of child abuse, and you tend to have violent episodes, you may find some counselling useful in helping you break out of this cycle of violence. There are also self-help groups that may also be useful. If you have been in previously abusive intimate relationships and you tend to gravitate to these relationships, take the same advice: seek counseling and break out of this pattern of violence.

## A NOTE OF INTEREST

Having identified the violence perpetrated by women against men, I, in no way, want to downplay or equate the amount of violence that women suffer at the hands of men to the violence of women towards men. In fact, the world over, women are seen to be the recipients of extreme forms of violence, and this is the case today in most parts of the world. Men are still beating and humiliating their spouses and girlfriends at an alarming rate. This has to stop. It is no longer acceptable; but then, **all violence must stop!**

# CHAPTER 19 - REFERENCES AND FURTHER READING

Abraham, S. (2005). "Yes, Women Do Abuse" – MenWeb – Men's Voices Magazine – Retrieved September 5, 2005, from organization's website at *http://www.menweb.org/scottwom.htm*

Brothers, B. J. (2001). *The Abuse of Men – Trauma Begets Trauma*. New York: Haworth Press Inc. Also, co-published in Journal of Couple Therapy, 10(1).

Boxall, H., Roseveau, L. & Payne, J. (2015). Domestic violence typologies: What value to practice. *Trends and Issues in Crime and Criminal Justice, 494*. *http://www.aic.gov.au/publications/current%20series/tandi/481-500/tandi494.html*

Dodich, C. & Siedlaz, M. (2014). Date rape drugs. International Journal of Child and Adolescent Health, Supplement, Special issue: Management of Substance Abuse, 7(4), 355-368.

Goldenson, J., Gaffner, R., Foster, S. L. & Clipson, C. R. (2007). Female domestic violence offender: Their attachment security, trauma symptoms and personality organization. *Violence and Victims, 22*(5), 532-545.

Pryor, D. W. & Hughes, M. R. (2013). Fear of rape among college women: A social psychological analysis. *Violence and Victims, 28*(3), 443-465.

Raphael, A. (2013). Rape is rape: How denial, distortion, and victim Blaming are fueling a hidden acquaintance rape crisis. Chicago, Illinois: Lawrence Hill Books.

Swan, S.C., Gambone, L. J., Fields, A. M., Sullivan, T. P., & Snow, D. L. (2005). Women who use violence in intimate relationships: The role of anger, victimization, and symptoms of posttraumatic stress and depression. *Violence and Victims, 20*(3), 267-285.

Weissman, D. M. (2007). The personal is political – and economic: Rethinking domestic violence. *Brigham Young University Law Review, 2007*(2), 387-450.

# CHAPTER 20

# "MY PARENTS NAG ME"

## PARENTS AND TEENS IN CONFLICT

One of the more frequent complaints of young people is "My parents nag me". Sometimes, it is "Mom" or "Dad", and sometimes both. Sometimes, it is Grandma or a step-mom or step-dad. On the other side of the picture, parents and other guardians often complain that young people won't do homework, won't clean up their rooms, and won't acknowledge curfew. This last-mentioned complaint is usually for those between 15 and 17. "That's all I ask him to do, and he won't do it!" was the comment of one parent. It is no wonder that some parents are accused of nagging, because they are continually saying the same thing, "Go do your homework!", "Go clean up your room!", or "Get in on time."

## PARENTS DON'T SEE THIS AS NAGGING

Interestingly, many parents do not see this as nagging, but only as having to remind their youngsters to do the same thing over and over. As one parent put it: "If the work was done in the first place, I wouldn't have cause to mention it again and again."

## YOUTHS NOT TAKING RESPONSIBILITY

Although times have changed over the past twenty or thirty years, parents and young people are still at odds because many young people refuse to take care of their responsibilities at home. However, the conflict has become more strongly voiced on both sides, and this often leads to unpleasant situations.

## DIDN'T FEEL LIKE IT

I recently asked a fifteen-year-old why he wouldn't do his homework, and he replied, "I didn't feel like it." On closer scrutiny, I discovered that he didn't feel like doing it, because he couldn't do it. Some young people don't like cleaning their rooms because it is work, and our society tells us that we shouldn't like work.

## SOME YOUTHS SEE JUST CAUSE FOR NAGGING

However, if you were to ask several young people why they think their parents nag them, they would give a similar and surprising answer. Despite the fact that they complain about being nagged, and may even express dislike for their parents, they will confess (if their parents won't know about it) that their parents are really nagging them for their own good. A young girl, about fourteen, when asked why she wouldn't do what she was supposed to, and why she let her mother worry and talk so much, told me jokingly, "That's what kids are for." She wasn't taking the 'nagging' seriously, and so she wasn't really doing anything to change the situation. In the meantime, her mother continued to worry.

## PARENTS WANT BETTER PERFORMANCE

Many parents continue to worry and make demands simply because they want their young people to perform better. Parents are continually telling young people to do homework, because doing homework is one of the ways young people learn. When young people don't do homework, especially when they need to learn and practice certain concepts at home, they are really fooling themselves, not their parents. Parents nag their children about cleaning their rooms, because parents want their children to know how to take care of themselves and their surroundings. If young people are as sophisticated as they want others to think they are, then they should take action to change their behavior and become more responsible. Eliminate the situations that cause conflict and there will be an end to the nagging. This is how the parents I interviewed felt about their nagging.

## YOUTHS CAN'T SEE OPPORTUNITY

Many parents 'nag' because they are frustrated by the inability of their children to see opportunity. This is often because parents, though having the ability, may not have had the opportunity to pursue their own dreams. Many have made sacrifices of their own careers to ensure that their children have the opportunity to realize their own dreams, and in some cases, the dreams their parents never realized themselves. Many parents have also made great achievements and want their children to do the same or better. Think of the frustration and the disappointment of parents who have sacrificed only to find out that their children either do not have dreams or else are not making the best of the opportunities they have.

## A WORD OF ADVICE TO YOUNG PEOPLE

Show your parents that you appreciate their concern. At times, their nagging may become too much, but think about it. How would you feel if you were in their position? If your parents nag you about cleaning your room, why not surprise them and clean your room when they least expect it? Guess what?

## NEW IMAGE OF YOU

They will very likely start looking at you in a whole new light. This could be the starting point to gaining their respect. If your parents nag you about homework, do it, even before they remind you. You will have to face your teacher the following day anyway, and that could be embarrassing, too. If you have problems understanding your work, talk to your teacher, and later talk to your parents. Even though most parents demand perfection of their children, parents are not perfect themselves, and will work with you to become the best person you can be!

## DON'T OPPOSE CURFEWS

On the question of acknowledging curfews, young people should recognize that this is important. With instances of innocent young people getting hurt or killed mistakenly, or the case of being in the wrong place at the wrong time, many parents confess that they are nervous when their children go out, and can only rest easily when they know their children are at home. Also, with so many abductions of children, of young people, and even of adults, taking place each year, it makes good sense to keep your loved ones informed of your whereabouts. If you don't acknowledge your curfews, and come in whenever you want, then your parents do not know if everything is fine with you. Parents worry a great deal about their children, so the least young people can do is to respect the curfews that their parents set for them.

## BE CONSIDERATE AND CALL

If there is some reason why you cannot be home by curfew, then the considerate thing to do is to call home and inform your parents of your delay. Then, later, on arriving home, explain more fully your reason for not being home on time. Maybe your parents may quarrel with you for not setting out early enough to be home on time, but they are only doing so out of worry and concern for you.

## ALSO, SIGN OF RESPECT

Most importantly, though, keeping curfews is a sign of respect. You live in your parents' home, and even if you are eighteen or older, you need to show them respect. If you follow the rules and do what is expected of you, chances are your parents won't have to tell you the same thing over and over, and there would be no need for "nagging".

# CHAPTER 20 - *REFERENCES AND FURTHER READING*

Borders, L. D., Black, L. K., & Paisley, B. K. (1998). Are adopted children and their parents at greater risk for negative outcomes. *Family Relations, 47*(3), 237-241.

Mindszenthy, B. & Gordon, M. (2005). Parenting your parents: Support strategies for meeting the challenge of gaining in the family. Dundurn Press.

Pincus, D. (2016). Irresponsible children: Why nagging and lecturing don't work. Empowering Parents. Retrieved from www.empoweringparents.com/article/irresponsible-children-why-nagging-and-lecturing-dont-work

Schenk, P. W. (2002). Teens, teach your parents to stop nagging. Retrieved From *http://www.drpaulschenk.com/articles/nagging.htm*

# DEALING WITH STEPPARENTS

With the high rate of divorce since the 1960s, many of our families are reconstituted families, or families made up of parents, stepparents, children, stepchildren or various combinations of these. This has more or less become a norm in our society. As reconstituted families try to normalize their relationships, problems sometimes surface that threaten the new marriages and families. Young people are often hurt in the process. However, increasingly, many divorced parents realize the importance of maintaining stability for their children, and they are taking steps to ensure their new relationships last.

## HALF-TRUTH JUST AS BAD AS UNTRUTHS

Problems often come about because of bitter ex-spouses. Either ex-husband or ex-wife may try to spite the other parent, and this often involves one parent making it very difficult for the child to see the other parent. Besides, in many cases, bitter things are said, sometimes untrue, to turn the child against the other parent. Sometimes, half-truths are told and these could be just as bad as untruths. Omitting important elements of a story could also wreak havoc with parent-child relationships. One parent may often undertake this strategy of telling half-truths to make the child dislike or think less of the other parent. In anger, the one parent may try to spite the other parent, not realizing that he or she is really creating conflict for their child.

## WHEN PARENTS DON'T COME BACK

There are also situations where one parent left and did not come back. In some cases, the parent that left may not have wanted any entanglement with the other parent. Sometimes, the hurt was so much that the parent preferred to leave everything behind, until the child was old enough to have an independent relationship with the parent that left. At times, the parent that has left may have been prevented from having a relationship with the child, while the child may have been told that the parent did not care, or did not want to have a relationship with the child.

Some parents may have neglected their children who were left behind, while others may have thought about and may have been missing their children every day for years. In many instances, children do not have accurate information of what may have happened, or even if they do, they may be unable to understand their parents' experiences.

## CHILDREN AND YOUNG PEOPLE MAY CAUSE DISRUPTIONS

Some parents are able to deal maturely with the ending of their relationship, but some children are unable to understand or accept it. When some of these children become part of reconstituted families, they may sometimes cause serious disruptions. They may reject a new spouse for their parent, and may sometimes create much stress in the marriage, giving rise to a second divorce. Some children make unreasonable demands on parents, hoping that their parents would disrespect or discard their new spouses or relationships to meet the demands of their children. Many young people give their parents an ultimatum: "Choose your new spouse or choose me!"

## COACHING BY EX-SPOUSE

An ex-spouse may coach his or her children and young people to be disruptive to the other parent's new family life. Sometimes, children are unable to deal with the break-up and with the fact that they may be used as pawns in the wrangling that continues to take place between their parents. Sometimes, both parents, though divorced, try to help their children to live as normally as possible, but some children mistakenly try to spoil the new lives of both their parents, with the hope that their parents would get back together. This is often an impossible dream that neither parent may entertain or even desire.

## ACCUSATIONS AGAINST STEP-PARENTS

Then, there are the new relationships that develop. Children can very easily accuse stepparents of any manner of ills. Children often do not have to say very much to have stepparents accused of dislike, abandonment and jealousy. This is particularly true of stepmothers, where the archetype of the wicked stepmother looms large in children's fairy tales and stories, and even in the plot lines of some adult fiction. At the same time, this is not to discount the fact that there may be genuine cases of dislike, abandonment and jealousy. Yet, there are many stepmothers who love and care for their stepchildren as though these children were their own flesh and blood, only to find out later that they are hated and despised by the very children they loved and nurtured.

Even so, this is no reason for stepparents to dislike their stepchildren. Giving love to stepchildren is a responsibility and a gift to the stepparents who have the ability to give love. Even if the love is not reciprocated by stepchildren, stepparents have nothing to be ashamed of or to be angry about. Their ability to love is to their credit. Shame on those who do not recognize it!

## IGNORANCE OF SITUATION

Part of the problem that afflicts our society is that of ignorance. Many children are too young, or too shocked, by the break-up of their families, to understand what may have happened in their parents' relationship, even if they were given accurate information.

## GREATER INSIGHT WITH AGE

However, as children grow older, they usually gain greater insight. As children move into adolescence and start forming their own intimate relationships, they become aware of the many things that could go wrong, and that may have gone wrong in their parents' relationship.

As many experts tell us, adolescence is the time when many young people come face to face with the inaccuracies they have been living with. For the first time, many adolescents face the fact that their divorced parents are never going to get back together. These adolescents may also realize that the divorce was the best thing that could have happened then. For the first time, many young people wonder what may have brought their parents together, because they may see how very different and incompatible their parents really are.

## SOME YOUTHS CONTINUE HOSTILITIES

Unfortunately, on the other hand, many adolescents may continue to take sides, continuing hostilities that they know ought to have ended years ago.  In some cases, many adolescents feel guilty for not being with the absent parent all those years, and in order to 'make it up' to that parent, may create distance and even hostilities towards stepparents that may have loved and cared for them, while their natural parents were missing.

## DON'T BOTTLE UP YOUR NEGATIVE FEELINGS

If you are a young person who is having a difficult time sorting out your feelings towards your custodial parent, your stepparent, and/or your natural parent who is absent, do the smart thing.  Talk it over with a parent or an adult. At times you may need to talk it over with a professional or a neutral party.  If your feelings are causing you difficulty in focusing on your school work, speak to your school counsellor or social worker, who would either help you resolve your feelings, or would refer you to more appropriate counselling, if this is warranted. Don't bottle up your feelings, for they could only hurt you.

## SPEAK TO YOUR PARENTS AND STEPPARENTS

Speak to your parents and stepparents, and let them know what you are experiencing because of the relationships they have. Remember, you do not have to wait until you are in crisis to seek help.  Having a good and healthy relationship with your parents and stepparents would most likely make your life happier, and would make the significant others around you happier as well.  One day, you may be a parent, and you would be able to provide for your child a strong, healthy family life, without animosities, where he or she could prosper emotionally, having the support of people who love him or her. Besides, hostilities from one generation often carry over into future generations, if these hostilities are not dealt with adequately.

## HEALTHY FAMILIES THAT LOVE EACH OTHER

Increasingly, many young people are living in very healthy relationships with their parents and stepparents, where their parents and stepparents get along, and provide a strong support system for their children. Many parents realize that if they are to be fair to their children, that although they may not get along as spouses that they could agree on being united in their parenting role. Many of these parents who are in second marriages, realize that they need to be respectful to their new spouses and that they need to include these spouses in all areas of their lives. These parents are able to build links that create happy, extended families for all concerned.

# CHAPTER 21 - REFERENCES AND FURTHER READING

Cartwright, C. (2010). An exploratory investigation of parenting practices in stepfamilies. *New Zealand Journal of Psychology, 39*(1), 56-63.

Christian, A. (2005). Contesting the myth of the "wicked stepmother": Narrative analysis of an online stepfamily support group. *Western Journal of Communication,* 69 (1), 27-47.

Dunn, J. (2004). Understanding children's family worlds: Family transitions and children's outcome. *Merrill-Palmer Quarterly, 50*(3), 224-234.

Ganong, L. H., Coleman, M. & Jamison, T. (2011). Patterns of stepchild: Stepparent relationship development. *Journal of Marriage and Family, 73*(2), 396-413.

McCarthy, J. B., Edwards, R. & Gillies, V. (2003). *Making families: Moral tales of parenting and step-parenting.* Durham: Sociology Press.

Stewart, S. D. (2010). The characteristics and well-being of adopted stepchildren. *Family Relations, 59*(5), 558-571.

Van der Pas, S., van Tilburg, T. G. & Silverstein, M. (2013). Stepfamilies in later life. *Journal of Marriage and Family, 75*(5), 1065-1069.

CHAPTER 22

# WHY LEAVE HOME?

Why are young people running away from home?  In an article I wrote some time ago to explore the possible reasons why young people leave home, I was very pleased, yet saddened, by the number of calls I received on this topic. I realized then that this was a problem much bigger than I had anticipated. I heard from parents as well as from young people who had previously run away from home. One interesting observation was that 8 out of every 10 calls I received came from women, either mothers or daughters, which is not to downplay the situation that boys also run away from home. When fathers called me, they spoke about the relationship between their wives and their daughters.

## ABUSE MAJOR REASON FOR LEAVING

One of the most common observations from the calls that I received from daughters was that some young people leave home because of abuse: physical and emotional.  Some young people leave because of continual conflict among family members, particularly with parents.   From the parents' perspective, some of the reasons for conflict were that young people were being influenced by friends, wanted "to have their own way", or had probably become involved in a drug, sex or gang culture.  Many of these reasons were also the ones I found in researching this topic, except that sexual abuse was also noted as a factor in the literature on runaways. Following are some interesting insights that both young people and parents shared with me.

## "INCLUDE MY THOUGHTS"

One young woman, 21, who had left home several years ago under very difficult conditions, asked me to be sure to include her thoughts in a future article, because she felt it was important that both young girls and mothers heard what she had to say. Her life as a runaway was a very difficult one, and four years after running away from home, she was on her own, but now with two young children, one child two and a half and the other 9 months. When she spoke to me, she was getting back into school to get her high school diploma.

According to this young woman, parents usually have the opportunity to deal with the problem before it escalates and gets out of hand. She explained that there are always 'symptoms', because young people "do not just get up and decide to run away. I didn't." Parents either choose to ignore these symptoms or else are not tuned into their children enough to recognize these. One of the major 'symptoms' is that the young person is not happy. According to this young woman, "Happy homes make happy children. If children are happy, they won't run away." This was her experience.

## PARENTS DO NOT FACE REALITY

Another caller pointed out that she believed parents often do not want to face reality, and they sometimes behave as ostriches, hiding their heads in the sand. This caller was a parent who realized after her daughter had left home that there were signs that she did not want to face. In fact, she pointed out that before her daughter left home, the young girl had threatened to run away on several occasions, but she didn't take her daughter seriously. Some of the other behaviors that her daughter displayed were isolation, staying in her room whenever she was at home, not taking part in family activities, sometimes not speaking to her parents for days, not bringing friends home, displaying anger inappropriately, and 'picking a fight' whenever she could.

According to this mother, she thought it was a phase that her daughter was going through, but in retrospect, she noted that the situation had been deteriorating for years. She didn't want to recognize it for what it was.

## EMBARRASSED BY PARENTS

Another young woman who had run away from home not very long before reading my article pointed out that she was very unhappy at home, and one of the reasons she mentioned was that her mother did not 'respect' her. She explained that whenever the phone would ring, her mother would pick it up, and would question the caller before giving her the phone. Even when the daughter wasn't at home, her mother would question callers and embarrass her. Most of her friends were aware of this, and many stopped calling her. This was 'the straw that broke the camel's back', but there were many other issues. Being embarrassed by parents seems to be a major issue for many young people.

## DIFFERENT DEFINITION OF ABUSE

Another caller explained that many parents 'abuse' their children, and do not recognize what they do as abuse. At times parents beat their children or slap their young people, thereby humiliating them. Other parents see spanking their older children as something within their right. According to one parent, parents should 'not spare the rod and spoil the child'. However, one caller, a young woman, who spoke of 'abuse' was not speaking about physical abuse. She was speaking about the emotional abuse that takes place when a parent calls a young person 'stupid' or merely implies that their child is. Or when the parent shouts at the young person, or sometimes makes a scene in public.

This caller explained that for a long time she thought she was stupid because of how her parents treated her. Some of the most powerful things we communicate are not in words. The way we look at someone, the way we ignore, avoid, or pretend that the other person is not there, are all ways that we communicate how we feel about others. Many parents do not recognize this as abuse.

## NEED FOR INDEPENDENCE AND MORE

As children become young people, they crave independence. This is a natural occurrence. The problem arises when they seek too much independence too soon. At the same time, many parents forget that their children are approaching maturity, and that these grown children need to learn to make decisions for themselves.

## YOUNGSTERS MUST EARN TRUST AND RESPECT

However, if young people do not show their parents that they are becoming more responsible, that they could make fairly mature or good decisions, then it is unlikely that parents would consider their young people responsible. In other words, young people have to earn the trust and respect of their parents.

## ESCAPING DIFFICULT SITUATIONS

Some young people see running away from home as a way of escaping difficult situations. From the calls that I received, one of the main factors was that some girls believed they were old enough to make their own decisions, and did not have to follow their parents' rules, particularly their mothers'. In many instances, the rules were quite routine, like doing chores around the house, not staying out without getting permission, and not being disrespectful and talking back to parents and other adults. Some girls perceived having to carry out these rules and having to do chores as difficult. They believed that by leaving home they could avoid helping out around the house, and escape the arguments that were sure to erupt with their parents, particularly their mothers. Many of these girls saw running away as the solution, because in many instances, they reasoned that they would be able to make their decisions for themselves.

## HOLDING PARENTS HOSTAGE

Some young people run away because their parents do not do what the young people want them to do, and they see this as a signal that their parents don't care. Others see it as a control issue. Other young people know the truth, namely that their parents are not being unreasonable, but they try to make their parents feel guilty. By making their parents feel responsible for their unhappiness, many young people hold their parents hostage to get whatever they want.

## PARENTS HAVE MIXED REACTIONS

Parents had mixed reactions about their children's running away. One mother explained that when it first happened, she was very 'nervous' about her daughter, not knowing where she was. When she did find out where her daughter was, she was anxious, knowing that her daughter may be easily led astray. One father who called pointed out that he went through a similar range of emotions. He was worried at first, then angry, and then disappointed. He explained that he still had a mixture of these feelings on occasions, even after a year.

## PARENTS WANT CHILDREN HOME AGAIN

From what these parents said, it is clear that they love their children and would do anything to have their children home again. Some parents expressed disbelief that their children would actually leave home, literally running away. Some parents were shocked that their children would want to leave home, knowing how much their parents loved and cared for them. Many parents confessed that there were signs, but they often ignored them, believing that their children were not serious about threats, and that their children were only going through a phase that would soon pass.

## WHAT YOUNG PEOPLE OFTEN THINK

It appears that while parents want to do right by their young people, they sometimes do not know when things are going wrong. On the other hand, many young people expect that their behavior would signal to their parents that they are not happy. Sometimes parents do not read the signs accurately.

## WHY VERBAL COMMUNICATION IS SO IMPORTANT

Verbal communication is very important. If parents ask questions when they see their young people acting strangely, this may be an opportunity for them to have an honest conversation with their children. If parents keep an open mind when speaking with their children, listen carefully, and respect their children's feelings, it is likely that changes can be introduced that would defuse difficult situations.

Similarly, children can let their parents know when they are unhappy. They might also find out that their parents may also be unhappy. Honest communication could reveal many situations where action can be taken to stave off more difficult relationships. From conversations I had with parents and with young people, I truly believe that if honest communication had taken place, if parents and their older children were not speaking at each other, that they may have heard the pain that each side may have been experiencing.

## LEAVING HOME MAY NOT BE AN OPTION AFTER ALL

Therefore, young people, if you are having any challenges with your parents, do not assume that your parents are aware of these. They may still be seeing you as their little child that they understood long ago, and may not be realizing that you have grown into an adult or near-adult that needs more independence. Start a respectful conversation with your parents and probably you may not even see leaving home as an option.

# CHAPTER 22: REFERENCES AND FURTHER READING

Brown, T. L. & Amundson, N. E. (2010). Youth experience of trying to get off the street: What has helped and hindered. *Canadian Journal of Counselling and Psychotherapy (online)*, *44*(2), 100-114.

Dey, J. G. & Pierret, C. R. (2014). Independence for young millennials – Moving out and boomeranging back. *Monthly Labor Review, 137*(12), 1-10.

Ferguson, K. M. (2009). Exploring the psychosocial and behavioral adjustment outcomes of multi-type abuse among homeless young adults. *Social Work Research, 33*(4), 219-230.

Pacifici, C., White, L., Cummings, K. & Nelson, C. (2005). Vstreet.com: A web-based community for at-risk teens. *Child Welfare, 84*(1), 25-46.

CHAPTER 23

# WHY YOUNGSTERS NEED NOT LEAVE HOME

## WHOSE FAULT IS IT?

However, I should add that parents should not have to take the full blame for this. Parents are often doing their best under very difficult situations. Besides, parenting is not always easy, and it is a 24-hour, 7-days-a-week responsibility. There are no manuals that could be consulted when a difficult situation arises, and so parents have to draw from their experience as children to determine how to deal with the situation. With times changing, parents often do not know what to do.

## YOUNG PEOPLE NOT ALWAYS INNOCENT

Speaking to parents, I gathered that young people are often not the innocent ones they are thought to be. They are often well aware of how to aggravate and manipulate their parents. Young people may be unhappy at home, sometimes because of situations that exist. However, in many instances, young people help create these very situations. Maybe a young person insists on staying in his or her room all the time. Parents may quarrel with him or her about this. The young person may decide to continue doing so, knowing that it is aggravating to the parent. This may be the only way the young person feels that he or she could get back at parents. This may be a ploy to justify running away from home.

## CAN'T HAVE THEIR WAY

However, there are times when 'getting back' at parents may not be because parents are abusive, but because young people cannot have their way. A parent's demand for his teenage daughter to "get off the phone" may be more serious than the parent realizes, because the person on the other side of the phone may be, in his daughter's eyes, only the most gorgeous boy in school. For the teenage girl, having to get off the phone just as she was getting the young man interested is a catastrophe, and she swears she would never forgive her father for this, because she knows that her dream date may never call her again. The young man who impresses everyone in school and is popular feels like crawling into a hole, when his mother shouts to him while he is on the phone: "Get off the phone!!" In the whole scheme of things, this may appear quite trivial to parents, but in the life of this young person it may be the most important thing at that point in time. In fact, in one situation, a young girl left home because her mother did just this.

## PARENTS THOUGHT 'ONLY A PHASE'

One parent noted that there was no indication that her daughter was thinking of running away from home. She had not been really breaking rules, but she was very angry. An only child, she scarcely talked to her parents. They thought she was going through a phase that would soon pass. It wasn't a phase.

# SOME REASONS GIVEN FOR RUNNING AWAY FROM HOME

However, as many parents pointed out, some of the issues that precipitated their young person's running away included repeated requests to do small chores around the house. One parent explained that a young person should see keeping his or her room clean as a 'normal responsibility', something that a parent should not have to ask a young person to do. Helping around the house should be a matter of 'courtesy and consideration', as another parent pointed out. Young people could show their appreciation to their parents by helping out.

## STAYING OUT LATE

However, another big issue that some young people and parents mentioned was that of staying out late. Many young people felt under pressure to stay out late, because there were other young people doing the same thing. On the other hand, many parents wanted their young people to be home at a certain time. The young people saw this insistence on being home "early" as an indication that their parents did not trust them, and that their parents were afraid particularly that they would become involved in sexual activity. As one young woman explained, parents were 'silly' about not allowing young people to stay out late, for whatever "we would do at night, we could very well do in the day, if we wanted to."

## PARENTS CONCERNED ABOUT SEX ND DRUGS

Many parents were gravely concerned about their children becoming involved in drug abuse and sexual activity. As one father called in, he and his son had a very good relationship and they did many things together. He explained he had season tickets for the hockey games, and he and his son always took in the games together. Then all that stopped when his son turned seventeen. His son hardly did anything with him. The boy's grades dropped dramatically, and he started skipping classes. According to this father, he felt that his son wanted to spend more time with friends, but he was not prepared for what he discovered.

## A FATHER'S SHOCK

One evening he decided to go up to his son's room to talk, and found him using drugs. "This was the beginning of the end," the father explained, for after speaking to his son harshly about the dangers of hanging out with the wrong crowd and using drugs, his son left home. He hadn't heard from or seen his son for almost a year. Then, little by little, his son began dropping by the house, but they were never able to rekindle the relationship they had before. This father lamented the fact that he did not intervene earlier, before his son had become so entrenched in the drug subculture.

## SELFISHNESS AND EMOTIONAL BLACKMAIL

One of the areas where some young people often demonstrate a great deal of hostility involves stepparents. A young girl who ran away gave her mother an ultimatum: "Choose him (her mother's new husband) or me." Her mother chose to remain married. According to this mother, her daughter resented anyone who received her mother's attention. The daughter failed to realize that her mother loved her just as much before as after she got married again. Some people may fault a parent for not choosing their child above another person. However, according to this mother, it is "pure selfishness" and "emotional blackmail" on the part of her daughter. This mother explained that she dated for a full year before getting married, and her daughter resented the relationship all the way. The mother thought things would improve after the wedding, but they didn't.

## COMPROMISE NEEDED

The message that seems to be coming out of this is that some young people try to make major decisions for their parents, without thinking of the repercussions for their parents and themselves. One of the biggest problems seems to be the need for communication, for parents and their young people to be honest with each other in a non-combative way. There is also a great need for compromise, and for not being selfish. These are issues that parents and their young people should consider carefully. Where there is continued conflict, they should seek counselling.

## FAILURE TO RECOGNIZE

Many young people sometimes fail to recognize the effort that their parents put into making sure things go well for them. Some parents make tremendous sacrifices, and sometimes are so consumed by what they are trying to do that they do not see what is happening to their children emotionally. Sometimes the everyday grind of making a living takes its toll on parents, and blinds them to the problems that are developing. Also, many parents fail to recognize the inconveniences that their children experience for them, especially in divorce situations, where parents prevent their youngsters from communicating with their other parent.

## EMPATHY FOR PARENTS

Although this is not a call to excuse parents, it is a call for young people to exhibit empathy, to realize that their parents are not perfect. Young people should recognize that their parents are often trying to be the best parents they could be, while at the same time trying to cope with difficulties in their own (the parents') personal lives. Young people could often make life much easier for themselves and for their parents if only they could be less demanding and more understanding. While young children could often be excused for not understanding what is going on, many young people often have the maturity to understand.

# RUNNING AWAY FROM HOME IS NOT ALWAYS THE ANSWER

Although home life could be very difficult, the answer is usually not running away. In cases of physical or sexual abuse within the family, a young person must get himself or herself to safety. Experts advise to report matters of abuse and not to hide them. Hiding abuse, especially sexual abuse and incest, would take its toll emotionally and would render a young person an emotional and psychological casualty over time. Some young people are afraid of reporting family members who abuse them this way. They fear that it would cause the family to break up. The fact remains that a family in which this activity is occurring is already broken up and dysfunctional, and in need of repair. A young person would not be keeping the family together by destroying his or her own young life. By allowing this abuse to remain hidden, a young person could be allowing other young people and children in their families to be abused in a similar way, and could thereby be endangering the safety and functioning of the whole family. This is something that could even touch the lives of yet another generation.

## RUN TO A SAFE PLACE

Young people who are experiencing sexual abuse or incest may find that they need to run to safety when they have the opportunity to do so. It would involve going to a place where help is available, and it is often with prior consultation. Simply running away to the streets is not wise, because running away means not having a plan as to where to live, and therefore exposing yourself to even further abuse and victimization on the streets. Speaking to an adult that could help you would often lead to finding a safe place to go. Then, you make a planned move.

## IT MAY NOT BE TOO LATE

If you are a young person who ran away from home, and you wished you hadn't, it may not be too late to make things right with your parents. Going back home may not be very easy, and parents may have been so hurt that they may want guarantees before they even consider you moving back home, if at all. They may want to have a relationship with you, but may prefer that you live somewhere else. Respect their decision.

## TRY TO IMPROVE RELATIONSHIP

If you are a young person who is not having a good relationship with your parents, try to improve it. See what is contributing to the conflict and address it. Speak to your parents and see how relations could be improved. Take the initiative to talk to them about what may be bothering you. Be polite! Nothing is gained by being argumentative or rude. Remember, although you may be a teenager or young adult, you are still a junior to your parents, and you need to show them respect. You cannot expect to disregard the rules of your parents' home. This could only cause conflict. You may need to make changes. Be reasonable and your parents would quite likely be reasonable with you. Before you know it, you could be having a rich and fulfilling relationship with your parents.

## BETTER AT HOME, IF NOT SEEK PROFESSIONAL HELP

From the calls that I received from some young people, as well as from research on the topic, life is usually much better at home than on the streets where young people have been beaten, sexually assaulted, robbed, pimped, and even killed. If there are serious problems at home, including incest and sexual abuse, seek professional help. It could start with a talk with a trusted adult, or your teacher, who is required to act on your behalf. It would likely lead to you leaving a home where you are being sexually assaulted and finding refuge, not on the street, but in a setting where your safety is ensured. From there, you can make healthy choices.

# CHAPTER 23: REFERENCES AND FURTHER READING

Cunningham, M., Wuthrich, V. & Davis, R. (2007). The Cool Teens CD-ROM: An anxiety management program for young people. *Journal of Family Studies, 13*(1). 104-106.

Dey, J. G. & Pierret, C. R. (2014). Independence for young millennials – Moving out and boomeranging back (2014). *Monthly Labor Review, 137*(12), 1-10.

Lieberman, L. & Lucas, M. (2013). Sport groups: Sports programming offered by Camp Abilities and the United States Association for Blind Athletes. *JOPERD – The Journal of Physical Education, Recreation and Dance, 84*(8), 16-23.

Osborne, V. (2008). Engaging kids where kids are at: The Eltham Library Project. *Australasian Public Libraries and Information Services, 21*(4), 178-181.

Oxford, M. L., Lee, J. O. & Lohr, M. J. (2010). Predicting markers of adulthood among adolescent mothers. *Social Work Research, 34*(1), 33-44.

Whitbeck, L. R., Hoyt, D. R., Johnson, K. D. & Chen, X. (2007). Victimization and posttraumatic stress disorder among runaway and homeless adolescents. *Violence and Victims, 22*(6), 721-734.

CHAPTER 24

# THE IMPORTANCE OF FAMILY

Old things pass away and new things take their place, but there are some things that maintain some stability. As families change in age, composition and structure, they continue to be important because of the emotional support they often provide. Even when families split, there can still be emotional support. This is an important point that should not be overlooked. Yet, in our society, where many of us may be immigrants, long-established or recent, we sometimes tend to overlook the significance of family. This is primarily because of the concept of family that we may now hold.

## EXTENDED FAMILIES

For those of us who have immigrated from different lands, we most likely have left behind long-established communities where our families lived for decades or even centuries. In those settings, our families included more than mother, father and children. Families included grandparents, aunts, uncles, cousins, and a host of good friends. Most of these lived close by. In North America, although we still see grandparents, aunts, uncles and cousins as family, they are often living in different cities, or are so far away that we may see them quite infrequently. It may even be the case that they live only minutes away within the same city, but we are still unable to see them often because of time constraints.

## ADJUSTING TO NEW LIVES

After years of separation brought about by immigration, many of us have been able to adjust to our new lives. Many of us have started our own families here, and many of these families have grown. Unfortunately, in many cases, our families often include the immediate economic unit: mother, father and children. Although we have friends, these seldom occupy the place of importance friends occupied in pre-immigration days.

## IMAGINE OLD FAMILY LIFE

For those young people who were born in North America from immigrant parents, they could only imagine what life was like then, and could never really experience and understand the bonding that took place in the villages and communities in their parents' homelands. They may argue that this is a new land and a new setting. We may even argue that these young people are more independent now, that they don't need to maintain the same close ties as before, and that there is no need for this sentimentality.

## EXPANDING OUR FAMILIES

However, there is a need to think of the importance of family, and it is necessary that we take a broader view of this concept. Family may extend to include very good friends, friends who are always there to support and encourage us, to rejoice with us when we are happy, and mourn with us when we suffer loss. We are also there, ready to support and encourage our friends, rejoice and mourn with them, as they do with us.

## WE WANT A PLACE TO BELONG

Regardless of how old or young we may be, and how independent we may feel, we all want to know we have some place where we belong, where we are considered a part. Families and friends provide that space.

## FAMILY AND FRIENDS – STRONG SUPPORT SYSTEM

Researchers are finding that individuals that have a strong support system tend to thrive better, and this is more so the case with younger people. It therefore seems necessary that particularly for children and young people we stress the significance of family, which includes not only blood relatives but our good friends.

However, there are times when families are terribly fractured. While efforts can be made to heal these fractures, sometimes the petty jealousies that may have caused the fractures loom large. In interviews that I have had with individuals, I discovered that in some instances, family members feel more comfortable with strangers than with their own blood relatives.

## A CALL FOR STRONGER FOUNDATIONS

However, the stronger a foundation we can build, the stronger a family we can sustain, whether with blood relatives or with good friends, the stronger a support system we would establish for our children, for our blood relatives, for our good friends, and for ourselves. If families become stronger, so would our society as a whole, for a fleet is only as strong and as fast as its weakest ship.

## CHAPTER 24: *REFERENCES AND FURTHER READING*

Baker, K. K. (2015). Legitimate families and dual protection. *Boston College Law Review, 56(85)*, 1647-1695.

Cook, K. (2014). The family: What is it? How do we study it and why? *Journal of Family Studies, 20*(1), 2-4.

Forsberg, H. & Natkin, R. (2016). Families in the future: Stories of Finnish students. *Journal of Comparative Family Studies, 47*(1), 1-31.

# CHAPTER 25

# RESPECT FOR, AND APPRECIATION OF, A VALUABLE RESOURCE

The wealth of a nation is dependent on the nation's ability to use its resources efficiently and effectively. Today, we must recognize that one of our greatest resources is human power. Regardless of the wealth generated by accumulations of oil, gas and other resources, it is human power that makes the difference. Human power, manifest in intent and action, could foster growth or bring about catastrophe. How we harness human power is therefore of the utmost importance.

## HUMAN POWER

This brings us to the human power we have available today. There is no doubt that children are important and count as the world's greatest resource. However, children need guidance now to become the human power that will lead generations in the future. Guidance requires knowledge in the present.

## IMPORTANCE OF YOUNGER ADULTS

We generally look for that knowledge in our adults, more specifically in our younger adults. We see these individuals as the ones that possess the know-how, the ones that are current, the ones that are on the leading edge of technology, the ones that are willing to push the envelope, and to see how far we could go. Our younger adults are the ones that are willing to take chances, and to experiment. These are the ones that are confident in their own youthfulness and adventure. This is good.

## BUT YOUNGER ADULTS NEED GUIDANCE

However, in being so preoccupied with youthfulness, being so assured of knowledge and abilities associated with youth, we fail to take into consideration that younger adults also need guidance. Some younger adults may think of this as absurd! Many younger adults or even people in their prime often fail to recognize the significance of experience, of contemplation and reflection, of patience and wisdom that our elderly have to share. In their haste to realize their dreams, many younger adults often disregard good counsel, mistaking it for the musings of the old. In accepting this, we, as a society, under-value one of the most valuable resources we have at present: our elderly.

## DON'T OVERLOOK OUR ELDERLY

We are so preoccupied with thinking of our elderly as feeble, senile, forgetful, and needful of rest, that we fail to recognize that there are some older people among us that do not fit this stereotype. Some of our elderly may not be as healthy as they once were, but many of them are healthier than some people half their age. Our elderly may be forgetful in some respects, but so are many younger people. Our elderly may be needful of rest, as are many of our young people.

## INTELLECTUALLY SOUND

Or again, many elderly people may not be physically strong as they once were, but they may be still intellectually sound. Many have the ability and the desire to carry out many useful functions in our society; and they have an invaluable wealth of knowledge to share. However, because of our bias against age, our ageism, we unwittingly discard this wealth. It is true that there are many retired people who want nothing to do with work. They have earned this right! But there are many who have knowledge that they would willingly impart to those who are willing to listen, and who respect that knowledge.

## MORE TO HUMAN POWER THAN INTELLECT

While we are conditioned to think of people in terms of being a resource, we fail to acknowledge that there is something far more important than being a resource to produce material things. After all, while being able to contribute to society in this way, there is feeling and caring of others that give us our humanity. Without our humanity, we would be nothing more than robots.

## FEELING AND CARING FOR OUR ELDERLY

Today, there are many retired people who feel lost, useless, and frustrated, when they recognize that they have so much to offer but that they are undervalued, seen as obsolete, at the very time when there is such a great need not only for the knowledge and good sense they could offer, but for the humanity they could contribute. Cultures that value and venerate their old often do not have the kinds of problems with their young that we experience in our society today.

## RECOGNIZING THE VALUE OF OUR ELDERLY

While our society devalues old age, as individuals we could do much to recognize the value of our elderly people. These are individuals that could provide good counsel, could tell us where we are going wrong, because they have passed this way before, and have encountered the potholes. These are individuals that are at a good place in life to benefit from hindsight, and to pass that on to us. Unfortunately, because of the stereotypes we have of older people, we tend to devalue the lessons they try to teach us, and make mistakes that we ought not to make, ignoring the good counsel that we are given.

## LET'S PAY ATTENTION TO OUR ELDERLY

Today, as we interact with our grandparents, older parents, and with older people in our society, we need to pay attention to what they are saying, and appreciate the wealth that they have to add to our lives. It may not be couched in high-tech terms, but if we really stop and listen, if we exhibit a willingness to learn, we may be pleasantly surprised to find out that they have the solutions to many of the problems that are afflicting us today. We may then realize how much our nation is shortchanging itself by failing to recognize our valuable resource: the elderly. Many indigenous peoples around the world venerate their elderly, while Western youth-oriented society tends to devalue our older population, to our detriment.

## LOVE, HONOR, AND RESPECT

More importantly, we should love, honour, and respect our parents, grandparents, and older people in general. Although some of them may lack the nimbleness that they once had, most have the same emotions they had when they were younger. They feel, they hurt, they love, and they want to be loved, in the same way that younger people do. Therefore, giving of our love and kindness, as well as our respect, is only one of the small things we could do to honour the elderly.

## ELDERLY AS HOLDERS OF WISDOM

Besides thinking of our elderly as a resource, we should therefore think of them as examples, as the source of wise counsel, and as the holders of wisdom. Despite the extraordinary innovations we are making today, if we ignore the knowledge of the past, we would be no better than a builder, who keeps constructing taller and more massive structures, while ignoring the foundation on which the structures rest. It would be only a matter of time before these structures all come tumbling down.

## *CHAPTER 25 - REFERENCES AND FURTHER READING*

Babb, T. V., Cenkner, L. A., Neal, K. A., Purk, J. K. & Sidell, N. L. (2010). The wisdom and vision of older adults: Changes in childcare since the Great Depression. *Sociological Viewpoints, 26*(2), 53-63.

Haslam, L. (2008). Occupational participation at 85 plus: A review of the literature. *New Zealand Journal of Occupational Therapy, 55*(2), 19-24.

Hatch, L.R. (2005). Gender and ageism. *Generations, 29*(3), 19-24.Martinson, M. (2006). Opportunities or obligations? Civic engagement and older adults. *Generations, 30*(4), 59-65.

Plikuhn, M., Niehaus, A. & Reeves, D. (2014). Sixty-five isn't what it used to be. Changes and trends in the perceptions of older adults. *International Social Science Review, 88*(3), 1-21.

Shukla, P. (2015). Spirituality and positive view of ageing in modern society. *Indian Journal of Positive Psychology, 6*(1), 122-126.

# CHAPTER 26

# THE AMBIGUITIES OF YOUTH

## UNRAVELLING THE CONFUSION YOUTH CAN BE A DIFFICULT PERIOD

Youth can be a particularly difficult period in the life cycle, both for the young person going through this stage, as well as for the adults who have to interact with the young person. The nature of the difficulty stems from the fact that youth or adolescence is a transitional or in-between stage, one that is fraught with many ambiguities.

## VARIOUS AMBIGUITIES ABOUT LOOKS

The ambiguities center around the fact that the young person may not be sure how to perceive himself or herself, sometimes seeing himself as a man, or herself as a woman, and sometimes as a child. Or the young girl may recognize that she is physically fully developed, but may not realize that she is yet emotionally undeveloped. There are also concerns for young people when they see their bodies growing unevenly, or their skins covered with acne. They worry about how things would eventually turn out.

## AMBIGUITIES ABOUT ABILITIES

Ambiguities may surface around the issue of wanting independence yet behaving in a manner that demonstrates dependence. Many young people believe that they are mature enough to do certain things, yet acknowledge that they are not mature enough for the consequences. Then, there is the peer group that exerts a great deal of pressure on the young person. Parents, seeing these inconsistencies, often question the sanity of, or the motivation for, their children's behavior.

## FOR EXAMPLE, MAN AND CHILD

In the first place, a young male may consider himself a man, and take this to mean that he does not have to respect the rules of the home. He may think of himself beyond curfews, and may argue that he is old enough to do what he wants. He may go to the extreme and tell his mother that it is his life and none of her business. He may even express the sentiment that he is a man now. Yet, there are times when this same young male behaves in a childish way, expecting his mother to take care of things that he should manage. He may not see anything contradictory in this, until his mother may point out that he cannot be a man and a child at the same time.

## PHYSICALLY DEVELOPED, EMOTIONALLY UNDEVELOPED

Secondly, a young female may recognize that she is fully grown, and consider herself a woman. She may decide that it is her life and she would do what she wants. This very likely brings her into conflict with her father, who may pronounce that there are certain rules in his house that have to be respected. Yet, this same young female may feel highly dependent emotionally and need the support of her parents, even though she behaves as though she doesn't care. She may be also plagued with how to deal with the emotional roller-coaster that is often associated with what constitutes appropriate behavior during this stage.

## INDEPENDENT V. DEPENDENT

Thirdly, there is the issue of independence and dependence. Youth is a stage when young people are eager to become fully adults, and when many of them want to take on the independent role. However, many young people are finding it difficult because they are still dependent on their parents for food and shelter. Even when these young people are able to get a part-time job, they find it cannot bring them independence. Those that leave home and go out on their own realize all too soon that independence comes with a price.

## EXTREMES OF TEMPERAMENT

Fourthly, the issue of maturity is raised as young people try on roles. This is the way that young people eventually decide which role suits them best, so there is much trial and error. For the adult, this could be distressing. One day, a young person may be totally compliant, helpful, loveable, and on the next, a completely different person. Some young people do not go through the extremes of temperament, but others do.

## MATURITY V. IMMATURITY

Fifthly, many young people believe that they are mature enough to do certain things, and may even take chances with breaking the law. When they are caught, they believe they are not mature enough to bear the consequences of their actions.

## FOLLOWERS V. LEADERS

Finally, there is the peer group. Many young people are followers, not leaders, and this is where problems arise. While they may want to behave independently and responsibly at home, when they go to school or out in the community they are faced with a different set of values. Those who are followers often succumb to subtle pressures to be part of the group.

## AMBIGUITIES – SOURCE OF QUARRELS

These ambiguities are the stuff of which great quarrels are made. Parents may get angry with their young people because of inconsistencies in behavior and because of broken promises over improved behavior. Many young people are confused as to what they are about, with all these different situations arising.

## MAYBE ALL IS WELL

Maybe you do not fall into any of these categories and you have a good and workable relationship with your parents. You recognize that there are times when you are expected to act as an independent individual and you do, and that there are times when you are dependent on your parents. You have conversations with them, and the ambiguities that affect some parent-child relationships do not affect you. This is good, and there are many young people who are able to avoid most of these ambiguities.

## TIME TO TALK AND THINK

What is needed is time to talk and think. Even if all seems right between you and your parents, it is a good practice to keep communication open. In this way, you prevent any opportunity for ambiguity. If you are one of those young people that experience ambiguities and are experiences quarrels with your parents, it is really time to talk and think. In many cases, a talk would go a long way to removing some of the uncertainties and fears that young people naturally have and which you may be having. Young people need to talk about any issues that cause them uncertainty or discomfort and this could take place in a comfortable, non-judgmental setting. Be open and honest with your parents about things that may be bothering you or leading to conflict with them. Although some questions may be difficult, still raise them and discuss them with your parents.

## PARENTS NEED HELP FROM YOUNG PEOPLE

In one of our parenting groups, a mother explained that one day when her teenage daughter asked her a question pertaining to sex, rather than answering it, she began accusing her daughter of being sexually active. As she told our parenting group, "She (the daughter) never asked me anything after that." Some parents feel uncomfortable speaking to their children about certain topics, but as another mother explained, when she has difficulty answering any questions, she usually gets her closest friend, another mother, to do it for her. She returns the favour and speaks to her friend's daughter. As this mother added, "you have to know and trust your friend." In this way, both mothers ensure that their children have all the right information.

Some young people may find it easier raising topics with their parents, while some parents may be afraid to raise certain topics for discussion, or may feel that their young person is not ready for certain discussions.

## YOUNG PEOPLE DO NOT HAVE TO BE CONFUSED

As a young person, you don't have to be confused about many issues. Parents sometimes do not bring up some issues, because they do not know how to approach them. However, if the issue is raised, most parents would respond. If you are faced with ambiguities that you are unable to deal with, what about opening up a conversation with your parents? You may be pleasantly surprised to see how supportive they could be!

# CHAPTER 26 - REFERENCES AND FURTHER READING

Brennan, M. A. & Barnett, R. V. (2009). Bridging community and youth development: Exploring theory, research and application. *Community Development: Journal of the Community Development Society, 40*(4), 305-310.

Paul, E. (2010). Why youth do not vote. *Canadian Parliamentary Review, 33*(2), 29-31.

Walsh, D. (2008). Helping youth in underserved communities envision possible futures: An extension of the teaching Personal and Social Responsibility Model. *Research Quarterly for Exercise & Sport, 79*(2), 209-221.

CHAPTER 27

# WHAT DO ADULTS EXPECT OF YOUTHS?

'Expectation' is an important concept. It means "the act of expecting or the state of being expected." When we have expectations, it means we are looking forward for results, and we can't be looking forward for results if we don't set the goals that we expect to be accomplished. When adults deal with youths, they must let youths know what their expectations of them are; if not, youths won't know what they are supposed to do. Very often, adults treat youths as individuals who cannot make a responsible contribution. This comes from the fact that adults often hold stereotypes of youths. Adults often think of youths as disrespectful, irresponsible, and unreasonable. Although many adults admit that there are those youths who do not fall into the stereotype, as a society, adults generally think of youth as having these characteristics.

## INADVERTENT MESSAGE

The message that many adults inadvertently send to youths is that they fit into this stereotype. Even when youths do not, they are assumed to be until they prove themselves otherwise. Probably, if adults take a different view of youths, expecting them to be respectful, responsible and reasonable, adults may be pleasantly surprised. Even those youths who have bought into the present stereotype may feel under pressure to live up to expectations.

## WHAT SHOULD BE ADULT EXPECTATION OF YOUTHS

What should adults expect of youths? - A show of respect, a sense of responsibility, and a demonstration of reasonableness. These are of vital importance particularly for today's youths. Decades ago, historians recognized the need for youths to take a prominent place in dealing with the ills of society. For example, Benjamin Disraeli, an English statesman and writer of the 19th century, declared: "We live in an age when to be young and to be indifferent can be no longer synonymous. We must prepare for the coming hour. The claims of the Future are represented by suffering millions; and the Youth of a Nation are the Trustees of Posterity."

### QUESTIONS ABOUT YOUTHS

What Mr. Disraeli said then is of even greater significance today. There are situations with some youths that are causing adults and youths from all walks of life to sit up and think, "What can we do to improve the functioning of youths in our society? What can we do to cut down on the amount of crime that is carried out by youths? How can we make meaningful change in our youth population?" Some may question whether there really is much youth crime. Regardless of how one may think, the fact remains that any crime is too much, and every effort should be made to reduce and if possible eliminate it.

## IS DEVELOPING PROGRAMS THE ANSWER?

Adults can develop numerous programs and can even have some youths take part in planning these programs. Some youths are already developing their own programs to reach out to their peers. Is this the answer? And what programs are being considered?

## CRUCIAL FACTOR

Society is overlooking one very crucial factor, and that is the minds of youths. Adults have to appeal to the minds of youths, impressing on them that adults have expectations of what it is to be a youth in the 21st century. Adults have to impress on youths, as Disraeli pointed out, that society can no longer consider "to be young and to be indifferent" are synonymous. Young people have to think seriously about how they would like the world to be and have to take a positive and proactive approach to developing our society.

## RESPECT FOR SELF AND OTHERS

Adults have to impress on young people that the urgency of the age requires that they have expectations of themselves, as adults have of them. Young people have to be respectful. This means having respect for themselves first. By respecting themselves, they would be guided as to what they can and cannot do that would help to maintain this respect. People who respect themselves behave in a way that earns them respect. They respect other people. They respect life. They respect the law, and they also respect authority. People who respect themselves behave in a respectful manner towards others, regardless of who those others may be. Adults expect young people to be respectful to themselves and to others.

## TAKE RESPONSIBILITY

Adults have to impress on young people that the urgency of the age requires them to be responsible. Young people have to take responsibility for themselves, and make the choices that would benefit them in the long run. They must take responsibility for their education and for their behavior. Young people have to recognize that they have a responsibility for helping to improve the conditions of others. In some instances, young people have to volunteer their services to help others. This is one of the ways that society can address the suffering in our communities.

## BE REASONABLE

Young people also have to be reasonable, to recognize that if they do not take steps now to improve themselves and the society in which they live, the world of the future would not be a very kind place for them to live and rear their families.

## HAVING EXPECTATIONS CAN CHANGE BEHAVIOUR

It is on this basis that adults have expectations for our young people, and adults expect them to have these same expectations for themselves. Young people must have respect for themselves and others, must develop a sense of responsibility, and must demonstrate reasonableness. Having expectations would go a long way to changing behavior. As a young person, you have a great responsibility to yourself and to your community.

# CHAPTER 28

# WHAT DO YOUTHS EXPECT OF ADULTS

Having written the article, "What Do Adults Expect of Youths." I thought it was only fair to do a follow-up article, "What Do Youths Expect of Adults." In order to obtain ideas for this article, I decided to get information from youths. Therefore, I asked a few young people to answer the question, in writing and unrehearsed, for me. These were the findings.

## SUPPORT, EXAMPLE, TRUST

One of the common responses to this question and in fact the one most frequently given was that young people want their parents to be there for them. One young man put it this way: "I expect my dad to be there when I get into trouble"; "I expect him to talk to me and give me advice"; "I expect my parents to trust me." This young man also said adults should be good examples for young people. Several young people wanted to be trusted and wanted their parents to spend time with them.

## ATTENTION AND RESPECT

Another response I got from a younger girl was that she wanted her parents' attention. One young man wanted his mother to allow him more time to spend with his friends, and another wanted to be able to bring his friends home, without his mother questioning them about him. Three of the responses did list respect as one of the things youths expect of adults.

## 'KIND' AND 'NICE' AND 'ACT MATURELY'

Another popular answer among teens was that adults should be 'kind' and 'nice' and not shout at young people. Several young people did say they expected their parents to buy them things and give them money ("lots of it"). One of the responses, though, that I thought was unusual came from an older girl, who wanted adults to be themselves, and to 'act maturely'.

## BE TRUTHFUL

While many of the responses dealt with parents, some dealt with adults in general. One young woman who responded had only one answer. I was curious and asked her to expand on what she had written. Basically, she told me she did not expect anything of adults. When I questioned her further, she explained that adults were not truthful: they often said one thing and did another. She found that adults often said things they didn't mean; and did things they shouldn't be doing. She was also concerned that adults were picking on youths, 'bad-mouthing them', when adults were often behaving worse than youths.

## NOT ALL YOUTHS ARE BAD AND IRRESPONSIBLE

I felt sad that such a young person was so cynical, but she was not bitter. She simply felt that adults just happened to be older, but they were doing many of the same things some young people were doing. What she didn't like was that young people were "getting a bad name", and older people were not being criticized for doing the same things, simply because they were older. "Not all young people are bad or irresponsible." Yet, many adults speak about young people as though they all are.

## SUPPORTIVE AND ACCEPTING

On thinking about the responses I got, I find that young people really appreciate it when their parents are supportive of their efforts. Young people want adults to be accepting of them, regardless of who they are. One young man tearfully explained that his parents do not accept him because of his sexual orientation. "I am the same person today as I have always been," he explained. Young people want attention from their parents, and they want their parents to trust them. They also want their parents to respect them. If adults disrespect younger people, how can they earn their respect? It is not enough to say, "I am an adult; you have to respect me." At one time, age was a criterion for showing respect. Although adults may still want this to be the case, young people are demanding more. They are demanding that adults set good examples, and that adults earn their respect.

## REMEMBER, ADULTS EXPECT TO BE TREATED WITH RESPECT

On the other hand, young people have to be aware of the way things were, of the respect that young people had for adults, regardless of who the adults were. Many of those adults today showed respect to their elders and expect the same treatment from the younger generation. Most adults today had good examples of what adults were supposed to be like, adults that respected themselves and others. Keeping this in mind, younger people should at least try to be respectful to adults, not because the adults may occupy positions of importance or influence, but because they are adults that respect themselves and others. Most adults deport themselves in a manner that is becoming of them. Therefore, younger people should not be looking for titles and accolades before they could show respect to an older person, or any person, for that matter.

## MUTUAL RESPECT

Young people are well aware of what they expect of adults, in the same way that adults know what they expect of young people. It is for individual parents and young people to communicate their expectations to each other, for it is in mutual understanding and appreciation that good relationships are forged.

## BE CLEAR ABOUT EXPECTATIONS

When adults are not clear about what they expect of their young people, young people can take the initiative and tell their parents, politely, what they expect from them. Young people can let their parents know, for example, that they value their parents' support and advice. Most parents would welcome knowing how they could be of assistance to their young people. Some parents are not as involved in their young people's lives, not because they don't care, but because they may not want to give the impression of controlling the lives of their young people. Young people can help by saying what they expect.

## WHAT IS YOUR ROLE IN THIS?

As a young person who may sometimes get into quarrels with your parents, or who may be concerned about your relationship with them, having a conversation about expectations can be a healthy approach to developing a stronger relationship. Most parents recognize that they must take a step backward and allow their children to prospect. It could be this same sentiment that causes parents to hold back from getting involved. At the same time, if you need your parents' support, ask them for it. Let them know that you welcome their support and consideration and ask them what their expectations are for you. In this way, you and your parents would be on the same page.

# CHAPTER 29

# BOUNDARIES NOT PRISON WALLS

Boundaries are limits. They are gentle reminders of how far we can safely go. Think of the rope that is put across a pool to indicate 'deep water' or of a sign saying that the beach is closed because of high levels of bacteria. These are examples of boundaries that indicate going beyond a certain point is prohibited. Generally, these boundaries are either to keep us safe or to prevent us from infringing on the rights of others. If you are a young person, parents and other guardians set some of your boundaries. Your school sets other boundaries, and the law sets others. These boundaries limit how far you could go in your behavior.

## BOUNDARIES: PARENTS AND GUARDIANS

Boundaries set by parents or other guardians are usually for your safety, but to listen to the way some young people describe these boundaries, one would think they were behind prison walls. Some of the boundaries may entail how late young people may stay out, how long they may stay on the phone, what evenings they may go out, whose homes they may visit, and if they have a part-time job, how many hours per week they may work. Some young people find this very restricting, and sometimes get angry with parents or other guardians for setting these boundaries.

## CONSIDER REASONS BEHIND BOUNDARIES

If you are a young person in this situation, think about the boundaries that your parents or guardians have set for you. Consider the reasons behind these boundaries. You would find in most cases these boundaries are intended for your safety. Going out late in the evening could put you in the wrong place at the wrong time, so that you may be the recipient of unwanted behavior, or be accused of displaying unwanted behavior. Spending too much time on the phone could cut into your study or homework time, and could also deprive others of the use of the phone. Going out every evening or working too many hours could also deprive you of study time. Keeping the wrong company could also jeopardize your safety. Parents or guardians quite likely considered all of these possibilities when setting these boundaries, because they care about you, and not because they are trying to ruin your fun or your life.

## BOUNDARIES: SCHOOLS

Schools also set boundaries. There are specific times that students must arrive for the start of class, and in many instances students are not allowed to leave school premises during hours of school. In some cases, students are required to wear uniforms. Most schools have a zero tolerance for any kind of violence. Arriving late for school consistently, or being absent from class and hanging out in the nearby mall or video arcade, or demonstrating violence, physically or verbally, could bring serious consequences for students who fail to recognize these boundaries. If you find these boundaries very restricting, think about the reasons behind them. You would realize that they are there for your safety. They are also there to prevent you from infringing on the rights of others, and to prevent others from doing the same to you.

## BOUNDARIES: THE LAW

The law has set boundaries for your behavior as well, and just as the boundaries set at home and at school should be respected, in the same way the boundaries set by the law should be respected. You are not allowed to drink or smoke, if you are under age. Driving is allowed only with the proper permit or license, and in some instances with a suitable instructor, or with other duly licensed driver. Drinking and driving do not mix. To combine these activities is not only breaking the law, but it is also not a very smart decision. Again, if you look very closely at the boundaries set by the law, you will see they are for your safety and the safety of others.

## BOUNDARIES HAVE A PURPOSE

As an intelligent young person, you realize that although you do not like boundaries or restrictions, they are there for a purpose. Without boundaries, we would have chaos. Therefore, start with observing the boundaries set in your own home. As the saying goes, "Charity begins at home." If you can learn to live by the rules in your home, recognizing what your parents or guardians stand for, even though you may not agree with them, you would find you are more likely to abide by the rules at school. Observing the law is important for in some instances failing to recognize these boundaries could literally land you behind prison walls.

## LEARNING TO OBSERVE BOUNDARIES

Learning to observe boundaries would stand you in good stead as you become an adult, for in everything we do, there are limits. Many of these limits are to protect us, some to prevent us from infringing on the rights of others, and some to prevent others from doing the same to us. We cannot always have our way or do what we want, if in doing so we infringe on the rights of others. Living in a civil society means that we have to compromise, and we have to recognize boundaries.

# CHAPTER 30

# HAVING GOOD INTENTIONS IS NOT ENOUGH

Many years ago, as a teenager, I was a victim of good intentions. The reason I want to share this very personal experience with you is that if you are a parent, a guardian, a teacher, a community worker or a teenager, there may be lesson here for you.

## EARLY LIFE

Having completed high school in the Caribbean, I was awarded a scholarship to attend university in New York City. It was a great opportunity, and I really appreciated it. There is no doubt, in afterthought, that the scholarship committee had intended not only that I should receive the best possible education, but also that I should be the very best possible person, according to their definition, not mine. This was the source of my problems.

## CULTURE SHOCK

It wasn't long after I arrived in New York City that they set about to make me into a 'normal,' 'well-adjusted,' American urban youth. Of course, I couldn't be an American youth. I was just me. I was a youth, from a rural area, from a very small island with a very different historical background from the United States, and from a very religious family. I also had my own idiosyncrasies as an individual. In fact, at that time in my life, I had devoted myself almost exclusively to my studies, taking time out to attend church and engage in family activities. As far as I was concerned, I knew exactly what I wanted, and knew exactly how I wanted to achieve it. I had no time for anything else.

## THE GOOD OTHERS WANTED FOR ME

On the other hand, as far as the members of the scholarship committee were concerned, since I was not doing the usual things that American youth were doing, and since I did not have the same worldview expected of someone my age, they reasoned that there had to be something wrong with me. It was either that I had not developed emotionally as I should have and so I needed help, or else I was able to disguise my true self, pretend to be who I was not, while behaving in secret the way they expected an American youth my age to behave. They also had a stereotypical view of how a Black youth should behave. What they didn't know was that I had lived a simple life so far, that I had actually enjoyed that life, and that even in the face of opportunities for new experiences, I didn't want to change a thing. I was happy with the simple lifestyle I was used to.

## THE GOOD I WANTED FOR ME

In afterthought, the members of the scholarship committee did not have the facts. I had not told them what my life was like up to that time, or the fact that I was happy just as I was. They probably thought I would have liked being an American youth, and so set about the best way they knew how to make me into one. They did not enquire about my lifestyle either, but assumed that all youths had to think, behave, and have the same desires. They planned social activities for me to attend, and even went so far as to arrange a date for me. These were things that I was not interested in at the time. When I didn't fit into the stereotypical mould they had made, they reacted. Needless to say, this brought me into direct conflict with them.

## FAILURE TO SEEK HELP FROM OTHERS

I didn't write home about this because I didn't want to worry my mother. This was the first time I had left home, and it was difficult enough for my mother to allow me to go so many thousands of miles away on my own. I had images of her not being able to eat or sleep, worrying that I was so far away from home with no one for emotional support.

## WITHOUT SUPPORT, I DEVISED A PLAN

After several months of criticisms, questions, suggestions, insinuations, and restrictions by the scholarship committee, I decided that I had had enough. The member of the scholarship committee with whom I lived would question me about my friends, and at that point, I didn't even have friends. There was no opportunity. I could not stay after classes for any type of extracurricular activities. In fact, I had to choose my courses to be home by 5 p.m. every day! The scholarship committee invited me to their social activities, many of which I was not used to, and many of which I did not enjoy. When I found a church to attend, they criticized me on my choice of church, and even on my beliefs. Things were becoming unbearable, because I felt that I had no control over my life. I was drained emotionally.

## I THOUGHT IT WAS A GOOD PLAN

I decided to do something about this situation, and so planned to take action the only place where I had some control: in my schoolwork. I came up with a plan at the end of my first year at university. I knew that one of the conditions for maintaining my scholarship was that I had to achieve at least a B+ average. I figured that if I skipped my exams, and failed, I would be kicked out of university, and would be sent back home. No one would be the wiser. My mother required that I did my best in whatever I undertook, and if my best was not good enough, I knew she wouldn't blame me for not making it. Besides, my mother knew that I had always required the very best of myself.

## IMPLEMENTATION OF MY PLAN

I had begun to implement my plan. I had skipped five of my exams, when I received a call late one night from one of my professors, Mrs. Weinberg. She wanted to know why I hadn't come in for her exam that day. I don't remember what I said to her on the phone, but she told me to come in to see her the following day, which I did.

## DISRUPTION OF MY PLAN – EMOTIONAL INTELLIGENCE AT WORK

I told her everything – my plan and all. Although she was a middle-aged Jewish woman - from a different cultural background, a different ethnic group, a different generation, and a different religion - she understood what I was going through, and she told me what I needed to hear at that point in time. She encouraged me to hold on to what I believed, and she showed me how my plan was going to hurt no one else but me. After our conversation, I agreed that my plan had to be scrapped, that I was going to be me, regardless of what others thought. She advised me to contact my other professors and make up the exams. However, before I left her office, she had made the calls, explained the situation, and made arrangements for me to make up the exams I had skipped. This was a very good thing.

## OLD ENOUGH, BUT STILL NEEDED HELP

One may say that I was old enough to make my own arrangements, and that was true, but in my emotional state at the time, there was no way I was going to contact any of my professors. She recognized this. I am very thankful that there was someone who was insightful enough to try to find out what was happening in my life, and who was there to help me over the difficult times, when I wasn't able emotionally to help myself. I always think back that if this intervention had not taken place, my life would have been very different from what it is today. As Maya Angelou would say, this woman was the 'rainbow' in my clouds, or my 'angel'.

## WHEN DIFFERENT PERSPECTIVES CLASH

In retrospect, from an adult perspective, I realize it was not that the members of the scholarship committee did not care about me. They did. The problem was that they had their ideas about what was good for me, not paying attention to the fact that I too had my own sense of self, that I knew who I was, and what I wanted. Despite the fact that they cared, the message that I was receiving from them was that something was wrong with me. Their intentions were good, but wrong for me. At the time, from my youthful perspective,

I felt they were trying to ruin my life. I couldn't see beyond this!

## GOOD INTENTIONS, BY THEMSELVES, ARE NOT ENOUGH

From my talk with my professor then, I realized that I had to think 'survival'. By keeping my goals in mind, and dismissing the distractions and obstacles, I learned to survive. Therefore, from personal experience, I came to realize that good intentions are not enough. Good intentions must be tempered with good sense, with empathy, and with a desire to allow individuals to develop naturally with guidance and with good advice. I also came to realize that there has to be a willingness to share our feelings and experiences with others.

### FOUND MY CALLING

Over the years that I have been working with young people, I have found, and am still finding, many in the same predicament I was in. Some situations are more stressful; others not. Some young people are failing school not because of lack of ability, but because this is where they have control, where they could escape difficult situations, and where they believe they can hurt the adults that hurt them inadvertently. Some young people are conscious of what they are doing; others are not. Some are failing school simply because they have given up and don't care anymore.

# WHEN ADULTS TAKE THE TIME TO UNDERSTAND YOUTHS

There are many adults who take the time to find out what is happening with the young people around them, and who are able to provide a listening ear when this is necessary. They also recognize when a young person is looking for help or advice, or when that young person simply needs someone to be there in a supportive role, someone to believe in him or her.

## WHEN YOUTHS DO NOT COMMUNICATE

It is also true that young people could be difficult, but there are many young people who do not communicate how they feel. They expect parents and other adults to know this. The truth is, many adults are far removed from the mindset of young people in their care.

## MY MISTAKES AS A YOUTH

When I was a young person, the mistake I made was keeping quiet. I should have spoken up and let the members of the scholarship committee know how I felt and how they were hurting me. If I had done this, very likely matters would not have escalated to the stage that they did, and I would not have been hurt the way I was. It is also possible that the scholarship committee could have found me a challenge, not knowing what and how I was thinking, and why I had such a simple lifestyle. In fact, one member of the scholarship committee had said something to me that reverberates even to today, and which got me thinking that I had to take control of my life. She said, "I have to know what you are thinking, even before you think it!" I thought then that there was really no one that would have so much power over me that they would be able to know my thoughts to such an extent. This made me share even less with anyone. They had no idea of my simple lifestyle up to that time.

## WHEN ADULTS MAKE WRONG ASSUMPTIONS ABOUT YOUTHS

Looking back at my situation now through adult eyes, I can see that the scholarship committee only wanted what was good for me. They went about it the wrong way, because they made wrong assumptions about who I was and what I wanted in life. I made the grave mistake of not speaking up, and not sharing my ideas with them.

## ARE YOU LIKE I WAS

If you are a young person in a similar situation today, recognize that the reason your parents or adults may seem to be picking on you is not that they hate you. In most cases, they want what is best for you, and may not even be aware that you are seeing their actions as interference. Parents, in particular, could so desperately want what is good for you, or want so much to make sure that you don't make the same mistakes that they did, that they overreact at times.

## FORGIVE WELL-INTENTIONED ADULTS

If your parents or adults have hurt you, forgive them, for that was most likely not their intention. Talk to them. Let them know how you feel. Let them know that they are hurting you, for many of them may not even be aware that this is the effect they are having on you! Some of them may be trying to survive emotional hurt themselves and are hurting you in the process. Let them know what you want for yourself.

## SHARE YOUR PROBLEMS WITH PARENTS/ADULTS

You may also have problems that you are dealing with, and parents won't know except you tell them. It is possible that the problems you are experiencing outside of home are also causing you to behave in ways that cause conflict in the home. You need to talk about this, so that your parents could be supportive of you with whatever difficulties you are experiencing. Speak to your parents or to other adults who could give you good advice, provide a listening ear, or furnish the help you need. Although you may think you know all there is to know, you don't, for years bring experience and wisdom, and you may have a long way to go. Even older adults are still learning, and will continue to learn for the rest of our lives.

## GIVE INPUT – YOUR IDEAS ARE VALUABLE

At the same time, as a young person, your ideas are valuable, because you can bring fresh perspectives on old issues. Always communicate your feelings, for adults around you may be unaware of these feelings, and with good intentions, could hurt you without even realizing it. Let them realize that having good intentions is not enough.

## COMMUNICATE, BUT DON'T BE HURTFUL

However, in communicating with your parents and other adults, don't be hurtful, even though you may be hurting. This could only lead to more hurt on both sides, and could aggravate rather than ameliorate the situation. Be gentle in expressing your hurt, and in doing this you may find your parents and other adults are better able to accept what you are saying without putting up defenses or without trying to explain why they are right and why you should not be hurting.

# MORE READING AVAILABLE

If you found this book beneficial, you may also want to consider trying out some of the other books in this series. See the back of the book for details. You may also want to send us comments at info@IsraelinShockness.com.

"Thanks for reading! If you found this book useful, please post a short review where you obtained this book. I read all the reviews personally so I can get your feedback and make this book even better."

Printed in Great Britain
by Amazon